luscious berry desserts

luscious berry desserts

BY **LORI LONGBOTHAM**

PHOTOGRAPHS BY **JAMES CARRIER**

CHRONICLE BOOKS

SAN FRANCISCO

First thanks to Bill LeBlond, Amy Treadwell, Judith Sutton, Emma Star Jensen, George Dolese, Elisabet der Nederlanden, and James Carrier. Many thanks to Jerry Goldman; Steve, Liz, and Sarah; Auntie Jean; Ellen McGill; and the Perrys.

My gratitude for good times and first-rate humor to Deborah Mintcheff, Barbara Ottenhoff, Barbara Howe, Jean Galton, Marie Regusis, Leigh and Joanna, Sabra Turnbull, Sarah Mahoney, Carol Kramer, Lisa Troland, Rosie and Sprocket, Val Cipollone, Tracey Seaman, Jim Standard, Jennifer Gregory, Sharon Bowers, Mary Goodbody, Tish Boyle, Kathy Blake, David Bailey, Amy Albert, Kim Masibay, Debby Goldsmith, Susan Westmoreland, Cathy Lo, Rosanne Toroian, Susie Quick, Frances Largeman, Eileen Runyan, Lisa Comegna, Jena Myers and her parents, Moira Dixon, Scott Smiley, Robert Martien, Herb and June, and Jon and Debby.

Library of Congress Cataloging-in-Publication Data available.

ISBN 0-8118-4414-5

Manufactured in China.

Designed by Lux Design. Prop styling by Emma Star Jensen. Food styling by George Dolese and Elisabet der Nederlanden. Typesetting by Lux Design.
The photographer wishes to thank Kevin Candland, his studio partner, who through his selfless and tireless efforts helped make their new studio ready in record time for its first assignment: this book.

Distributed in Canada by Raincoast Books
9050 Shaughnessy Street
Vancouver, British Columbia V6P 6E5

10 9 8 7 6 5 4 3 2 1

Chronicle Books LLC
85 Second Street
San Francisco, California 94105

www.chroniclebooks.com

Page 2: Lime and Thyme Blueberry Pound Cake, page 29

for SARAH NAULI LONGBOTHAM—
you're the berries!

Berries, eh? There's good cheer when there's berries.
CHARLES DICKENS, *The Haunted Man*

Contents

berry delicious

*Berries are stunningly gorgeous and elegant,
they combine well with other dessert "makins," and
everyone adores them. In fact. no fruits are
more well loved or better for you than beautiful berries.
Or more versatile—these small wonders
are the crown jewels of the fruit world and
one of nature's greatest gifts. Within each
berry lies a multitude of different flavors and
textures that can be drawn out to do whatever
you, as a cook, want them to do.*

I'm the first to admit you don't need complicated or fancy recipes for berries. Simply pile plump ripe berries in a beautiful bowl and add plain or flavored Custard Sauce (page 151), thick cream, a dollop of sweetened or unsweetened Crème Fraîche (page 153), or a big spoonful of whipped cream. Or toss them with a Fabulous Flavored Sugar (page 155), such as lemon verbena or ginger. A bowl of strawberries on the stem served with bowls of sour cream and brown sugar was the height of sophistication when I was a child. Now I might choose crème fraîche and dark Muscovado sugar, with its toffee-like flavor.

But there are other delights here too, a little more complicated than berries and cream or custard, that give great rewards for the small amount of time you spend putting them together: Lime and Thyme Blueberry Pound Cake (page 29), Raspberry Truffle Tart (page 46), Marionberry Brown Betty (page 94), Roasted Strawberry Shortcakes with Vanilla-Scented Biscuits (page 62), and many others. I think you'll be very happy with them.

While I love desserts, I don't really like just sweetness without a contrast to it. Sweet and tart, sweet and bitter, even sweet and hot make me much happier than just sweet. And that is the very reason I adore berries and berry desserts. (And the reason I'm crazy about lemon desserts and dark chocolate desserts.) Ripe berries naturally have a good balance of sweet and tart, and berry desserts present a freshness, a beauty, and a celebratory feeling offered by few others. Think blueberry pie at Labor Day or strawberry shortcake on the Fourth of July.

Luscious Berry Desserts offers recipes using the berries I consider to be the big four—strawberries, raspberries, blackberries and their cousins, and blueberries. The recipes are flexible, and berry substitutions are encouraged. Please use what you have, the more local the better, depending on where you live and what's growing nearby. There are no cranberry recipes here because they aren't interchangeable with the other berries and they come to us in a totally different season. And I haven't included recipes for gooseberries or fresh currants, because they are only rarely available to us.

While I recommend berries at the top of their game, at the height of their season, I must say that many times in the last several years I've been drawn, way out of season, to the fragrance of ripe berries in my local greengrocer—and have been very pleased with the berries after getting them home. I do believe there are berries around much of the time that can make us surprisingly happy, even if the calendar tells us they shouldn't be so good.

One of my most memorable mornings ever was picking strawberries with my friend Barbara on a warm summer day in Maine. We literally lay down among the berries, picked dozens, and ate more. We were giddy and exhilarated at the thought of actually getting all the strawberries we wanted, and slightly guilty at the pleasure. For who has ever *really* had enough strawberries? There is no doubt strawberries are best eaten in the patch—the warmth from the sun makes them even more lush and juicy. But if you don't have a handy patch, try local farmers' markets for very fine berries. When berries are sold near to where they grow, it means the fruit has been allowed to ripen fully on the bush, which increases both the sugar content and the flavor tremendously.

It would be very difficult for me to choose one as my favorite berry. My most beloved seems to be the one I'm eating, cooking, or thinking about at the moment. I'll think of raspberries, and I'm sure they are my favorite. Their flavor explodes in my mouth and is as big as it gets.

But then I think of strawberries: there is nothing better than the simple bliss of eating strawberry desserts—shortcakes, ice creams, pies, and tarts. Just their faint come-hither fragrance can fill me with memories of simpler times, and finding a whole patch or punnet that is strawberry through and through, and none with tasteless, wooly white centers. Ripe blackberries and all their cousins have great flavor, with a perfect balance of sweet and tart, and are amazingly juicy. They remind me of rural life, berry gathering, and living totally with the seasons. Then there are blueberries. What's better than a double-crust blueberry pie, a cobbler or a grunt, or warm blueberry sauce on ice cream? I can't, at the moment, think of anything.

Strawberries

When I was growing up, we had a small patch of strawberries outside our back door, conveniently located for grabbing a handful for morning cereal. I would dash out with my full bowl to top it with berries, and it was a little bit of paradise. Not only were the plants beautiful, with their graceful little white flowers, but the berries were warm and very fragrant in the morning sun. Tiny little things, they were big in perfume and flavor because that's what they were grown for, not bred for shipping. And because of them, I have always gravitated to small strawberries and am convinced that the smaller the berry, the sweeter and more intense their flavor will be. So, no matter where you get them,

look for small scarlet strawberries. And remember that local berries are riper, tastier, and less expensive than those that have more frequent-flier miles than you do. Also, the closer they are to market, the less damage they're likely to suffer in transit.

For me, strawberries are the "foremost" berry. They are almost everyone's favorite, but beyond being simply the best, in most places they are the first berries (and sometimes the first fruit) to appear each spring. They are the most widely grown of all berries, the glamour queen and summer's brightest jewel. Because of their radiant beauty, strawberries also make appealing fresh decorations and garnishes for just about any dessert.

Strawberries are members of the botanical family of Rosaceae, the rose family. They are one of the oldest fruits, and excavations of Swiss lakes have revealed strawberry seeds and fossilized berries dating from the Iron Age. In Roman times, both Virgil and Ovid wrote of gathering *fragra*, the old Latin name for strawberries and the root of its present generic name, *Fragaria*. (Their name says quite a bit about their fragrance.) The gorgeous heart-shaped fruits range from the tiny fingernail-size wild varieties to the extra-large cultivated strawberries, and their flavor varies according to variety and ripeness. An unusual and distinctive feature of strawberries is that the seeds grow on the outside of the fruit, rather than inside. The approximately two hundred seeds on the average berry give a certain very pleasant texture.

For centuries the only strawberries available were the tiny ultra-sweet wild ones. Those wild strawberries, or alpine strawberries, are called *fraises des bois* in French, meaning "strawberries of the woods." They have a pure flavor reminiscent of a combination of the familiar strawberry taste and vanilla. They are rarely cultivated commercially but can be found worldwide growing wild, particularly in forests. The sweetest strawberries, they are hundreds of years removed from the large varieties that have been developed since the mid-eighteenth century. The little white, red, or yellow berries are hard to find in this country, although they are grown on a small scale on the West Coast and are sometimes available in farmers' markets or upscale produce markets. You might grow them yourself.

The parents of all modern varieties were definitely from the Americas. Strawberries as we know them today are descended from two New World varieties. When the colonists arrived in what became Virginia, Native Americans were crushing and mixing the berries with meal to make bread. The delicate and flavorful woodland Virginia strawberry was taken back to Europe, where it was enthusiastically accepted. Another strawberry was discovered on the coast of South America by a French explorer. This one, a beach strawberry, firm and typically the size of a large hen's egg, had a flavor reminiscent of pineapple. When plants brought to France from Virginia were planted quite by accident next to plants relocated from the western shores of Chile, the unplanned hybrid of those two small sweet fruits, one red, one yellow, resulted in the much larger red-hearted, gold-seeded strawberry from which all others have been developed.

Until after World War II, strawberries remained a locally produced, limited-season crop. The big change came with a new variety from the California Agriculture Station in 1945, called the University variety, which had a longer season and could be shipped. Experimentation continues to come up with hardier, more prolific strawberries that produce fruit for a longer season and can be shipped long distances. Because they don't have to travel far, local strawberries can be picked when truly ripe, and that extra sun time increases both the sugar and vitamin C contents. The berries become darker, sweeter, and more nutritious. Commercially grown strawberries usually have a very firm texture with larger, tougher seeds. They are also somewhat denser and slightly less sweet than local varieties—but, even so, most commercial strawberries are better than good enough.

Strawberries are now grown in every state of the union, but the vast majority of the commercial crop, more than 88 percent, comes from California, where the season begins in January and can last into November. The best strawberries seem to arrive in the market in late May or early June and are well worth waiting for.

Strawberries beg to be eaten simply and, like all berries, have their fullest flavor at room temperature. Fresh cream is the classic accompaniment in England, where they are passionate about their strawberries, but a soured cream, called crème fraîche, is preferred in France. In Italy, and to some extent in France, red wine accompanies the berries instead of cream for the simplest of desserts;

Strawberries are beautiful, and it mars their beauty to cut straight across their tops to remove the green caps. You can use a little strawberry huller, which looks like a thick pair of tweezers, about 1 inch wide. Or use a sharp paring knife, inserting the tip under the cap at an angle and removing a cone-shaped piece of strawberry along with the cap.

freshly ground pepper might be added in France. Also in Italy you may encounter ripe red strawberries tossed with balsamic vinegar and sugar, a combination that can improve the flavor of less than perfect strawberries, although it may require an act of faith to try it the first time. (You will find the formula on page 137.)

If you are tempted to bake with strawberries, proceed cautiously. They lose their color and become soggy in batters. But baking them can be successful, as you will see in the Strawberry-Hazelnut Crisp on page 87.

Nutrition
Eight medium strawberries provide 14 percent of the recommended daily value of fiber, 7 percent of daily potassium, and 140 percent of the recommended daily vitamin C. Strawberries have more vitamin C than any member of the berry family. They are also a great source of antioxidants, phytochemicals, and folic acid, a B vitamin.

raspberries, blackberries, and their cousins

Raspberries and blackberries, like strawberries, are members of the rose family, and their stems have the thorns to prove it. They are also known as drupelet berries, because raspberries, blackberries, and their relatives have juice sacs called drupelets. Those drupelets are the characteristic that unites them and what makes them natural substitutes for one another in recipes and other culinary matters. And please do feel free to substitute raspberries in a recipe that calls for blackberries, or vice versa, or use any of the varieties of blackberries, such as loganberries, marionberries, and boysenberries.

Raspberries are the most fragile and therefore usually the most expensive of all berries. A bramble fruit like blackberries, raspberries have a delicate structure with a hollow core, so they have to be handled very gently and eaten as soon as possible after picking. Most raspberries are red, but some are yellow, apricot, amber, purple, or black. They have a very long season—California berries are available from June through October—and Chilean and other imports are available at other times of the year.

Raspberries have a big, big flavor that seems to explode in your mouth, and for me, they are as good as it gets. I love all berries, but I have always had a huge soft spot for raspberries. Aglow with color, with flesh like soft velvet, they remind me of a bowl of rubies. The extraordinary intoxicating aroma and intense essence of this deep red thimble-shaped fruit put me in a total swoon. Shy, their flavor is not. (I also like that their big flavor and sweet-tart balance allows them to stand up to chocolate.)

Indigenous to many countries throughout the world, raspberries are older than Christianity by centuries. The familiar red raspberry, primarily the achievement of horticulturists in Greece and Italy, has been commercially grown since the end of the sixteenth century. By the end of the nineteenth century, more than four hundred varieties were in cultivation, although the differences between them were very minor. Today, most of the older varieties have disappeared, because they are not suitable for commercial growing—meaning they don't ship well. Now most of the raspberries in this country are grown in the Pacific Northwest; California, Oregon, and Washington produce 90 percent of our raspberries.

Black raspberries, also known as black caps, are small, seedy, thimble-shaped berries that, like red raspberries, separate from the center core when picked. They are longer and firmer than red raspberries and have a vibrant purplish black to black color and a unique flavor. They can be tart or sweet, and the darker they are, the sweeter and juicier they will be.

Golden raspberries are the same species as the red and black raspberry but are softer, juicier, and sweeter, and often without the lovely tartness we find irresistible in berries. Some describe the flavor as a combination of raspberries, apricots, and bananas. For me, they are not at their best when cooked, but they certainly make a gorgeous garnish, and that's my favorite use for them.

I had a blackberry patch when I lived in Humboldt County, California. It was heaven. The vines were thorny, but the huge berries dripping with juice could be so good they actually helped teach me a bit of patience. Not a lot of patience, but I learned not to rush in and pick the unripe berries, which could be puckery and nippy, because just a day or so later, they would be perfect. The berries were a comfort, arriving every year in late summer and early fall. The earliest ones were the best and sweetest, and the later ones were "more pippy" and better for jelly. If you are serving them plain, pick the very ripest, juiciest berries, and add just a splash of cream and a sprinkle of sugar. If you're cooking with them, including a few underripe berries in the mix gives a lively tartness and seems to help with the thickening of the juices.

Blackberries have been cultivated only since the 1820s, but the varieties that have spread around the world are so numerous that some experts insist that it is possible to differentiate between two thousand separate varieties. They are grown primarily in the northern hemisphere and in the mountainous regions of South America. They come in many colors and shapes, with thorns and without, elongated and squat, and black to purple to gold to red. The most notable difference between raspberries and blackberries is the little hollow cup found in the raspberry, regardless of its color. When ripe, the raspberry lifts easily away from the white core, which remains on the plant, leaving the familiar hollow. The blackberry retains its core when picked. Blackberries have countless nicknames and aliases; in Britain they are called bramble berries. Their season is much shorter than raspberries, and here in the United States they are generally a late-summer, early-fall berry; they mark the end of the berry season. Following are some blackberry varieties, some hybrids, and other relatives.

The tayberry, a cross between a blackberry and a raspberry, was developed in Scotland. Tayberries have the best qualities of both parents, including the dazzling color of a raspberry, but they are not yet raised commercially.

Boysenberries are a thornless hybrid of either a blackberry and a raspberry or a dewberry or a blackberry, raspberry, and loganberry. Named for Rudolph Boysen, they are gorgeous, large (up to 2½ inches long), with large plump juice sacs, and velvety looking, with a vibrant deep purple color and a red glow. Succulently sweet, with a slight raspberry flavor, boysenberries are best when cooked. They make a stunning pie.

Loganberries are thought by some to be a blackberry and raspberry cross, developed more than a hundred years ago by a Judge Logan at his berry garden in Santa Cruz, California. More acid than a blackberry, they are large (approximately 2 inches long), slightly cone-shaped, and burgundy red, with a rich tart and tangy flavor. The loganberry is perhaps the queen of berries, bigger, juicier, and tastier than either a raspberry or blackberry. Grown commercially for their juice, the berries are great for pies, cobblers, and jams or for eating fresh. They do not exist in the wild.

Dewberries are trailing blackberries. They are similar to "generic" blackberries, but smaller, with a slight whitish bloom and a better, milder flavor. They also ripen earlier.

Youngberries are a cross between dewberries and loganberries. They look like a dark red, elongated blackberry, but taste more like a loganberry.

Olallieberries, a tart and sweet favorite for pies, come from Corvallis, Oregon, where George Waldo crossed a black loganberry and a youngberry in 1950. A good all-purpose berry, they are similar to black raspberries in appearance—long, slender, and firm, with large juice sacs and a shiny black color—and have a well-balanced flavor.

Marionberries are deeply colored with a full fragrance, a complex and intense blackberry flavor, and a fine balance of tart and sweet. A bright lovely berry with a dark maroon to black color, they are medium to large, elongated, and cone-shaped. They were cultivated in 1956 in Marion County, Oregon, where they still grow and are used in the superb marionberry jams and syrups produced there.

Cloudberries are golden or orange berries, related to the raspberry, which grow wild in Scandinavia, Arctic Russia, Siberia, northern Great Britain, and Canada. They are best for jam.

Although the elongated dark wine-red mulberries look like large loganberries, scientifically, mulberries are not related to blackberries or raspberries, and, unlike other berries, they do not grow on vines or bushes, but on trees. The beautiful dome-headed mulberry tree is a spectacular sight—they can grow to up to thirty feet across. Mulberries are glorious eating, sweet and flavorful, the true "eat 'em as you pick 'em berry." The mulberry is related to the fig, and there are black and white mulberry trees as well as red ones. White mulberry trees are used extensively in silk production (the silkworms feed on the leaves), but the red and black trees have better fruit.

Mulberries ripen later in the year than berries that grow on the ground. When ripe, they are very soft and juicy. Mulberries can be eaten as is, with or without cream, and they rarely need sugar. Use them as you would blackberries or raspberries; they are great in summer pudding, and in sorbets and ice cream. I have also enjoyed dried white mulberries in Turkey, where they are called *dut*.

blueberries

Blueberries come from a large extended family and are related to rhododendrons and azaleas. They were once called "star berries" because of their star-shaped crowns. Native to America, blueberries have been in existence for thousands of years. They were growing in New England when the first colonists arrived, and Native Americans taught them to dry the berries as a substitute for the raisins and dried currants they knew at home. One of the first North American explorers to mention blueberries was Samuel de Champlain, who in 1615 reached Luke Huron and reported finding Native Americans gathering blueberries for their winter store. But blueberries grow in many parts of the world. The Scots call them *blaeberries, blae* meaning blackish blue, and enjoy them as a jam for scones. They are also popular in Denmark and in the former Soviet Union, and are enjoyed by Eskimos in Alaska.

The berries are a dazzling bright blue with a slightly frosted look, called a "bloom." They begin as little green berries and become blue from their high anthocyanin content, the same compound that makes red wine red.

There are two main types of blueberries. The lowbush berries, also known as wild blueberries, are related to cranberries, huckleberries, and lingonberries. They grow in colder climes such as Maine, eastern Canada, and Minnesota; the bilberry is the European variety. Highbush blueberries, the cultivated berries, are grown from the East Coast to Michigan. Rabbit eye blueberries, related to highbush berries, are grown in the American South, but they are not an important commercial crop.

Not exactly wild, lowbush blueberries are not planted, but they are commercially managed by growers. They have a more complex and balanced flavor than the highbush berries, both sweet and tart, with an edge similar to the flavor of fresh thyme or the faint scent of pine. They are a darker shade of blue than their cultivated cousins, with a jet-black inside. Smaller and more fragile than their highbush relatives, these are not bred for shipping. Lowbush blueberries are difficult to pick, as they grow ankle high; they are harvested with rakes.

Highbush berries are sweet and plump with a silvery bloom. They can be up to four times larger than lowbush blueberries. Highbush berries are very easy to pick— they grow at a very convenient picking height, and you can strip a bush and fill a bucket in minutes.

Nutrition
At the U.S.D.A. lab at Tufts University in Boston, Massachusetts, researchers have found that blueberries rank number one in antioxidant activity compared to forty other fresh fruits and vegetables. According to scientists at the University of California at Davis, they may reduce the buildup of the so-called "bad" cholesterol that contributes to cardiovascular disease and stroke. A number of studies in Europe have documented the relationship between eating bilberries, the European cousin of blueberries, and improved eyesight, and a study in Japan found that blueberries helped ease eye fatigue. At the U.S.D.A. Human Nutrition Center laboratory, neuroscientists discovered that feeding blueberries to laboratory

rats slowed age-related losses in mental capacity, a finding that has important implications for humans.

Like other berries, blueberries are high in fiber, low in sodium, and high in potassium. One of the reasons blueberries have surged in popularity recently is they are on every diet from Weight Watchers to Atkins because of their low-carbohydrate, high-nutrition, high-antioxidant content.

berry basics

Buying Berries

Look for berries that sparkle; avoid any that are spotty, soft, or dull. They should appear moist and fresh and should not be withered, crushed, or dripping juice. And they should be plump, firm, well shaped, and uniformly colored. Wet berries are a sign of damage or possible decay. In the old days, we could look for juice stains on the bottom of the basket, or punnet, as they say in Britain. Now that is more difficult, as there's often a tinted absorbent pad on the bottom of the basket.

Choose berries carefully, as they may be packed in boxes that conceal inferior fruit beneath a display of perfect specimens on top, and one bad berry can quickly spoil the whole batch. If the box is not wrapped, you can remove a few of the top berries and peek beneath. And there shouldn't be any twigs or other debris. Always remove any plastic wrap as soon as you get the berries home; it can crush and bruise them.

Purchase strawberries that have a symmetrical shape and are firm and ripe, with a shiny flame-red to deep scarlet color. Avoid berries with any white, green, or yellow; pale greenish or yellowish fruit

is unripe and will be hard and sour, and strawberries with white shoulders or tips have not had enough sun to ripen completely. For best results, buy with your nose—aroma is a great indication of quality. The caps on strawberries should look fresh and bright green, and the berry tips should not look too seedy. Small berries often have better flavor, and I avoid the huge ones, which are often wooly and tasteless.

Strawberries are often picked before they are ripe, and although they may gain red color off the plant and look riper, they will not develop more flavor once they are picked. Still picked by hand, strawberries arrive in the market in pint baskets, twelve baskets to a flat (these "pint" baskets can actually vary in weight from twelve to sixteen ounces) or in clear plastic clamshell boxes. There are few moments more full of hope and possibility than taking home a flat of ripe strawberries.

If you're picking your own strawberries, always do so by cutting the stems. For best quality, pick berries that are fully ripe and at their peak of flavor, texture, and fragrance.

When purchasing raspberries, look for plump berries with a uniform dark red color; pale pink raspberries hold few pleasures. The berries should be firm, not soft or overly juicy. Because of their hollow core, raspberries are very delicate, so choose berries that are full and round, not flattened. The walls of a fine raspberry are full and meaty, and the berries shouldn't have any tiny dents or bruises or be broken. Superb berries have a hazy soft gloss to them.

Select blackberries that are glossy, dark colored, and well formed. They should be without hulls. If the hulls are still attached, the berries will likely be very tart and might not ever develop their full flavor. Avoid berries that are dull, dry, soft, moldy, or bruised. Blackberries are not ripe until every drupelet turns deep purple to black, they are soft, and they detach from the plant without bruising.

Choose blueberries that are plump, firm, and uniform in size and color; good blueberries look round and tight, not shriveled, and without dimples or dents. You shouldn't see any squished or bruised berries, mold, bits of plant matter or debris, or any leaking juices. Gently shake the container: firm berries will move freely, softer berries will stick together. They should be dark navy blue with the characteristic powdery, silver-white "bloom," a slight patina or dull gloss on their surface. Reddish blueberries are unripe and lack the flavor for eating raw, though they can be fine for cooking.

Locally grown blueberries are often riper—and therefore more fragile—than commercial berries, and they should be kept cool and used as soon as possible.

At Home
Berries are perishable, delicate, and precious, and, especially if they are burstingly ripe, you must treat them tenderly. When you bring home a box, remove any soft overripe berries for immediate consumption; discard any smashed or moldy berries, and very gently blot the remainder dry with a paper towel, then refrigerate immediately. Storage times for different berry varieties vary somewhat, but the sooner you eat them, the better.

Strawberries, raspberries, and blackberries are best if used within two days, but fresh sound blueberries, properly stored, will keep for up to ten days.

You want to handle berries as little as possible to prevent bruising. Berries are very sensitive to pressure, and optimum storage is next to each other rather than on top of each other, so they can breathe and won't crush one another. Spread out the berries in a single layer on a baking sheet or a shallow baking dish lined with paper towels. The paper towels absorb any moisture that accumulates, prohibiting mold growth.

It is best not to wash berries until just before serving, as moisture will hasten their decay. I don't always wash berries, especially raspberries, but when I do, I wipe them gently with a damp cloth or rinse them using as little water as possible. Dry the berries gently on paper towels. Then look over all berries again just before serving to remove any imperfect ones.

Strawberries are grown at ground level, so they may be sandy or dusty; I sometimes just brush off any sand. Leave the strawberry hulls on until after washing, so the berries won't absorb water.

Wash blueberries, just before serving, in a basin of cold water, and discard any twigs or leaves and unripe berries that float to the surface. Do this quickly—you don't want the berries to soak—and dry them gently and well. Or rinse them gently right in the plastic basket they came in, then tip them out onto paper towels to pick over.

frozen berries

Most berries freeze beautifully, which makes up some for their very short seasons. You might be happy buying ripe local berries at the height of their season and freezing them to use the rest of the year. It's better for many uses to have high-quality frozen berries rather than mediocre fresh berries. Most frozen berries can be stored for up to one year.

To freeze most berries, spread them out on a baking sheet and freeze them first, then pack in self-sealing plastic bags for long-term storage. Freezing the berries individually will avoid a hard block of berries. Blueberries can just be tossed into a self-sealing plastic bag and frozen, but do not wash them before freezing; it may make them tough.

If you have some overripe, soon to be past-their-prime strawberries, discard any damaged or moldy berries, puree the good ones, and, if not using the puree immediately, freeze it. Whole strawberries tend to turn mushy and unappetizing when frozen, so even if they are in good condition, when I have too many, I freeze them as a puree.

Buy frozen berries that are frozen individually, rather than in a syrup. Don't use any berries frozen in syrup in these recipes, or the desserts will be too sweet. When buying frozen blueberries, be aware that they can be huge, as large as quarters; if you find a brand that freezes tiny wild blueberries, make a note and stick with it.

When using frozen berries, it's not always necessary or advisable to thaw them first, but extra cooking time may be necessary if you do not.

baking basics

It's most important that you have fun, enjoy what you are doing, and not be anxious about the results. If your first efforts are not perfect to look at, you will find the encouragement to try again when everyone who tastes them raves about how delicious they are. You need not be a dedicated or experienced cook to produce delicious results.

All the recipes in this book are tried and tested, and changing the ingredients or methods will give different results. I suggest you follow the recipes carefully to begin with, and you will soon discover for yourself those that can easily be varied and how you might want to vary them.

Read the entire recipe before you begin. Then assemble the ingredients and equipment. Check to see if any ingredients need to be at room temperature before beginning.

Always use the best-quality ingredients.

Use the appropriate measuring cups for dry and liquid ingredients, and measure carefully. For liquids, use glass measuring cups with spouts. For dry ingredients, use metal cups that can be leveled off with a knife or spatula.

Preheat the oven for at least 15 minutes before baking. Be sure your oven temperature is correct; if it isn't, the baking time given in the recipes won't be reliable. Check the oven temperature often, using a mercury-type oven thermometer set on the middle oven rack. After preheating the oven, check the thermometer. If the temperature setting disagrees with the reading on the thermometer, adjust it up or down accordingly.

Baked goods should be baked in the middle of the oven unless otherwise indicated.

Most cakes, pies, and tarts should be cooled on wire racks (in or out of the pan, depending on the recipe) to prevent the bottom of the dessert from becoming soggy.

ingredients

Baking Powder and Baking Soda

Baking soda, pure bicarbonate of soda, is activated when it is mixed with an ingredient that is acidic, such as buttermilk. Baking powder, a combination of bi-carbonate of soda, cream of tartar, and cornstarch, works no matter what liquid it's mixed with, as the cream of tartar provides the acidity. Don't let a batter made with baking powder or soda sit around before baking it, or you may not get optimal service from the leavener. Check the expiration dates on the packages before using, and be precise in your measuring, as too little or too much will not give the desired result.

Butter

Opt for the fullness of flavor and the creaminess of butter when making berry desserts. Margarine doesn't taste good, it has an unpleasant mouth-feel, and it is loaded with trans-fats (the most unhealthy fats of all). Always use unsalted or sweet butter for these recipes; salted butter is too salty for berry desserts. (If you are observing Jewish dietary laws, you will want to substitute parve margarine for butter for nondairy meals. If you must use margarine instead of butter, use it in its least processed state; that is, don't use tub margarine, spreads, or butter substi-tutes, which contain more water than stick margarine and are not made for baking.)

Eggs

Use fresh Grade AA large eggs for these recipes; using a different size may mean disappointing results. Always purchase eggs from a refrigerated case and keep them refrigerated at home.

Pure Vanilla Extract and Paste

There is no quicker way to ruin a dessert than by using strong artificially flavored extracts. Vanilla—and other extracts—must be the real thing. No imitations. If you like to use vanilla beans rather than extract, you might consider trying pure vanilla paste. Vanilla beans, and their by-products, have become very expensive in the last few years, and rather than buying vanilla beans, and scraping out the seeds, and finding another use for the pod, I'm much happier using the paste. It is almost pure seeds and easily measured. Give it a try, especially if you find the look of the tiny vanilla seeds in your desserts irresistible. Nielsen-Massey makes one with beans from Madagascar that is available at Williams-Sonoma, Sur la Table, and other specialty foods stores. It's best to add pure vanilla paste or extract to cool ingredients since they have an alcohol base and heat will release not only the fragrance, but the flavor as well.

equipment

Baking Pans

Use shiny, not dark, baking pans. Baking sheets should fit into the oven with at least two inches of space between them and the oven walls so the heat can circulate freely.

Electric Mixers

I used a handheld mixer for every recipe in this book that calls for a mixer. If you have a heavy-duty standing mixer, feel free to use it, but you don't need one for any of these recipes.

Ice Cream Machines

There are now many reasonably priced machines available (at only about fifty dollars) that don't require the messy use of salt and ice, making the preparation of frozen desserts easy enough for a school night. Look for one that makes at least one quart.

Microplane

The Microplane rasp grater's razor-sharp teeth shave lemon and other citrus zest instead of ripping and shredding, and it removes a lot more of the zest than other graters and gadgets. It also seems to never remove the white pith, which is a minor miracle in itself (that bitter white pith may be great for making marmalade jell, because it contains a lot of pectin, but it can ruin a luscious berry dessert). The Microplane is very comfortable to hold and use, with a well-balanced design, like a good knife. Once you use one, you'll never go back. They are widely available in kitchenware stores; for more information, go to www.microplane.com. If you've ever left zest out of a recipe just because you thought it was too much trouble, give the Microplane a go.

Mixing Bowls

It's impossible to have too many mixing bowls. Stainless-steel bowls are great for using as an improvised double boiler over a saucepan of hot water. Glass bowls are essential for use in the microwave, for melting chocolate or butter. For dessert making, you'll need at least one very large bowl for beating egg whites, cream, and the like. I find deep bowls far more versatile than shallower ones.

Potato Masher

An old-fashioned potato masher is the perfect tool for mashing berries while cooking or mashing raw berries to release the juices. A pastry blender also works well.

Rolling Pin

The type you use is really a matter of personal taste; use whatever you feel comfortable with. Your grandmother's pin, a wooden dowel type, or a heavy ball-bearing pin with handles: any of these will be great.

Rubber Spatulas

One of the greatest recent advances in kitchen equipment is the development of heat-resistant rubber spatulas. Not having to worry about a meltdown is quite wonderful. So now you can use rubber spatulas for cooking, as well as for scraping down bowls while mixing, folding ingredients, and many other tasks. Very handy.

Sifter

I don't use a sifter for sifting, I use a coarse strainer. Use whichever you like, but for the best crumb and accurate measuring, don't skip the sifting step when a recipe calls for it.

Strainers

I use strainers often, to strain out tiny bits of overcooked egg and whatever else might get in the way of the perfect smoothness of a finished dessert. Have a few on hand, large and small, coarse and fine. You can use a coarse strainer for straining out raspberry and blackberry seeds because the seeds are large, but if you want a strawberry puree without seeds, use a fine strainer, because those seeds are tiny. A small fine strainer is also perfect for sifting confectioners' sugar or cocoa powder over a dessert just before serving.

Whisks

These are very handy kitchen tools. Find one that feels well balanced and comfortable in your hand. I often use a whisk to aerate and mix the dry ingredients; it's quicker and easier than sifting when sifting is not really necessary. I also use whisks for folding one component of a recipe into another. Have both large and small whisks on hand.

Wire Racks

A couple of large, sturdy wire racks are essential for cooling baked goods.

tips, techniques, and tricks of the trade

Beating Egg Whites

Always use an impeccably clean bowl and beaters. If I'm not absolutely confident that no vestige of egg yolk or other fat is lurking, I give the beaters and bowl a quick wash with a bit of vinegar and water. I've found it works best to beat at medium speed until the whites are foamy, then increase the speed to medium-high and beat to soft or stiff peaks as the recipe requires. For soft peaks, beat the whites just until when the mixer is turned off and the beaters are lifted the foam makes a peak that falls over immediately. For stiff peaks, beat until that peak stands straight up and stays there.

Cooking Times

When a range of cooking or baking times is given (for example, "Bake for 30 to 40 minutes") always check for doneness after the first increment of time has elapsed and then continue to watch closely until done.

Creaming Butter and Sugar

Use an electric mixer for creaming butter and sugar, and beat until the sugar is barely grainy and the mixture is light and fluffy. This can take a few minutes, so make sure to beat long enough. Begin with room-temperature butter.

Cutting Out Biscuits

Pat out the dough to the desired thickness. Dip the biscuit cutter into flour and cut out the biscuits using a straight in-and-out motion, dipping the cutter into the flour again before cutting out each biscuit. Then gather together and pat out the scraps if necessary to cut out more biscuits.

Folding

Folding is used to combine certain ingredients, such as whipped egg whites, with another ingredient or mixture without deflating them. Use either a whisk or a rubber spatula. First add a small amount of the mixture you're folding in to the bowl and cut straight down through the center of the mixture to incorporate it, then turn the whisk or spatula toward you and lift up. Turn the bowl an inch or two, and repeat, working around the bowl just until no streaks remain. Then add the remainder and fold in.

Measuring Brown Sugar
Firmly pack the sugar into a metal measuring cup, pressing down on it firmly enough so that it will hold its shape when turned out. Use a small metal spatula or a table knife to level off the top.

Measuring Flour
The way you measure flour for a dessert recipe is crucial to the final outcome. For these recipes, first stir the flour in the canister to aerate it, then spoon it into the measuring cup so that it mounds above the top and level the top with a metal spatula or table knife. (Always use a metal measuring cup for dry ingredients.) Dipping the measuring cup into the flour and scooping it out will give you a different amount of flour, and your results may be disappointing. Another flour caveat: 1 cup flour, sifted, is different enough from 1 cup sifted flour to affect the dessert. Pay close attention to whether the flour should be sifted before measuring or after, or both.

Preparing Cake Pans and Baking Sheets
For greased pans, just smear the bottom and sides with softened unsalted butter. If a pan also needs to be floured, add a little flour to the pan and shake and turn it so that the sides and bottom are covered with a thin coating. Then turn the pan upside down and shake out any excess.

Pureeing Berries
My favorite way of pureeing berries for a seedless puree is to pulse them in the food processor just long enough to break them up; longer processing can break open the seeds, and the insides of the seeds may give a bitter flavor to the puree. Then I pour them through a fine strainer if they are strawberries and a coarse strainer if they are raspberries, blackberries, or one of their relatives, and discard the seeds. The general rule is to use twice the volume of whole berries than the amount of puree you need—so if you need 1 cup puree use 2 cups of berries. But the amount and size of the seeds can vary, so err on the side of too many berries, rather than too few.

Rolling Out Pastry
Place the disk of dough on a lightly floured smooth work surface and sprinkle the dough and the rolling pin with flour. Roll out the dough with short, even strokes, working from the center out, lifting and turning the pastry as you roll. To transfer the pastry to the pan, carefully fold it over the rolling pin, lift it up, and drape it over the pan, then ease it gently into the pan without stretching it. For sticky or hard-to-handle doughs, flour a piece of wax paper and put the disk of dough on it, flour the dough, and place another sheet of wax paper over the dough before rolling it out. Using wax paper is also good if crusts make you nervous, and you need to build your confidence.

Preventing Blueberry Blue (or Greenish) Batter

· Rather than folding in the berries, place half of the batter in the pan, sprinkle with the blueberries, and top with the remaining batter.

· Coat the berries with flour to soak up their juices.

· If using frozen blueberries, fold into a batter, without overmixing, while still frozen for less breakage, and bake immediately.

· Use dried berries for thick, heavier batters where fresh or frozen berries may be ruptured.

Using a Pastry Bag and Tips

For the recipes in this book, you'll need only a good pastry bag and a basic set of tips. Choose a pastry bag that's a comfortable size for you. To use it, insert the tip you want to use, forcing it into the hole at the small end of the bag for a snug fit. Then fold the tip end up against the bag to keep what's inside from oozing out while you're filling the bag, place the bag tip end down in a large glass measuring cup, and fold the edges of the bag down around the outside of the cup. Using a rubber spatula, scoop the filling, frosting, or other ingredient into the bag. Remove the bag from the cup and twist the top closed. Hold the bag firmly with one hand just above the filling and use the other hand to guide the tip. Gently squeeze the filling out with the upper hand. I like using disposable plastic bags; the traditional canvas ones can be difficult to clean.

Cakes

This chapter offers a gorgeous assortment of berry cakes. Try the lovely four-story Lemon Layer Cake with Raspberry Curd (page 26) topped with a tangy lemon frosting—perhaps served with piles of fresh raspberries on the side.

Berries can give almost any cake a fresh taste and a delightful, delicate look. The flavors of cakes combine well with berries, and the textures are a great contrast. And berry garnishes are striking—just think of a vanilla or chocolate cupcake decorated with a dollop of whipped cream and a single blackberry or raspberry perched on a mint leaf.

There's also an intriguing cake with the scent and faint flavor of fresh rosemary, rose water, and blackberries (or the berry of your choice), Rosemary, Rose, and Blackberry Cake (page 32). Will the stunning and comforting Blueberry Upside-Down Ginger Cake (page 34) be your favorite? Maybe it'll be the Lime and Thyme Blueberry Pound Cake (page 29), packed with blueberries and topped with a refreshing and tangy lime glaze. There are recipes here to make everyone happy, and none are difficult to make or require special equipment or ingredients.

Lemon layer cake with raspberry curd

Celebrate birthdays, any occasion, or nothing at all with this luscious, dazzling cake.
A lovely light and tender cake flavored with lemon, layered with tangy raspberry curd,
and coated with a voluptuous lemony butter icing will make any day a happy one.

SERVES 8 TO 10

Cake

2 ⅓ cups	**cake flour**
2 ¾ teaspoons	**baking powder**
¼ teaspoon	**salt**
1 ¾ cups	**sugar**
2 tablespoons	**finely grated lemon zest**
¾ cup (1 ½ sticks)	**unsalted butter, at room temperature**
1 cup	**whole milk**
5	**large egg whites, at room temperature**
¼ teaspoon	**cream of tartar**
	Luscious Raspberry Curd (page 147)

Frosting

1 cup (2 sticks)	**unsalted butter, at room temperature**
2 tablespoons	**finely grated lemon zest**
3 ½ cups	**sifted confectioners' sugar**
3 tablespoons	**fresh lemon juice**
	Luscious Raspberry Curd (page 147)
	Ripe raspberries or mixed berries for serving (optional)

Continued

Lemon Layer Cake with Raspberry Curd

STEP 1: Position a rack in the middle of the oven and preheat the oven to 350°F. Butter and flour two 8-by-2-inch round cake pans.

STEP 2: *To make the cake:* Whisk together the flour, baking powder, and salt in a medium bowl. Pulse ¼ cup of the sugar with the lemon zest in a food processor until the zest is finely ground.

STEP 3: Beat the butter and the zest mixture with an electric mixer on medium-high speed in a large bowl until light and fluffy. Add the remaining 1½ cups sugar and beat until smooth. Add ¼ cup of the milk and beat just until blended. Reduce the speed to low and add the flour mixture alternately with the remaining milk in 3 batches, beginning and ending with the flour, scraping down the sides of the bowl with a rubber spatula as necessary, and beating just until blended.

STEP 4: Beat the egg whites with clean beaters on medium speed in a large clean bowl until foamy. Add the cream of tartar, increase the speed to medium-high, and beat just until the egg whites form stiff peaks when the beaters are lifted. Using a whisk or a rubber spatula, fold one-quarter of the whites into the batter, then continue to gently fold in the whites one-quarter at a time, being careful not to deflate the mixture. Divide the batter evenly between the pans and smooth the tops with a rubber spatula.

STEP 5: Bake for 35 to 40 minutes, or until a wooden pick inserted in the centers comes out clean. Cool in the pans on a wire rack for 10 minutes. Run a table knife around the inside of each pan and carefully turn the cakes out onto the rack. Turn them right side up and cool completely.

STEP 6: Hold the palm of one hand against the top of each cake layer and, using a long serrated knife, cut it horizontally in half. Place 1 of the layers on a serving plate. Spread the top with a scant ½ cup of the raspberry curd, leaving about a ½-inch border around the edge. Place another cake layer on top and spread it with a scant ½ cup raspberry curd in the same way. Repeat with another layer, using the remaining raspberry curd, and top with the remaining layer.

STEP 7: *To make the frosting:* Beat the butter and zest with an electric mixer on medium speed in a medium bowl until light and fluffy. Gradually add the sugar and beat until light and fluffy. Add the lemon juice and beat for 1 minute longer. (The frosting can be prepared a couple of hours ahead and stored, covered, at cool room temperature.)

STEP 8: Frost the cake with the lemon butter frosting. Cut into wedges and serve with the raspberries on the side, if using, or store in a cool place until ready to serve.

Lime and thyme blueberry pound cake

The thyme works a little magic by enhancing the flavor of the blueberries. Don't use large highbush blueberries for this cake, if possible; you'll be much happier with the small wild berries. You might instead use the tiny, intensely flavored dried blueberries—a generous cup would be perfect.

SERVES 10 TO 12

1 cup	whole milk
2 tablespoons	chopped fresh thyme
3½ cups	sifted cake flour (not self-rising)
½ teaspoon	baking powder
¼ teaspoon	salt
1½ cups (3 sticks)	unsalted butter, at room temperature
2¼ cups	sugar
6	large eggs
4 teaspoons	finely grated lime zest
1 teaspoon	pure vanilla extract
3 cups	ripe blueberries, preferably tiny wild blueberries, picked over
½ cup	fresh lime juice

Continued

Lime and Thyme
Blueberry Pound Cake

STEP 1: Position a rack in the middle of the oven and preheat the oven to 300°F. Generously butter and flour a 10-inch (12-cup) Bundt pan.

STEP 2: Bring the milk and thyme just to a boil in a small saucepan over medium heat. Remove from the heat, cover, and steep for 7 minutes, then pour through a fine strainer set over a bowl and let the milk cool to room temperature.

STEP 3: Whisk together the flour, baking powder, and salt in a medium bowl.

STEP 4: Beat the butter with an electric mixer on medium-high speed in a large bowl until light and fluffy. Reduce the speed to medium and gradually add 1¾ cups of the sugar. Increase the speed to medium-high and beat until the mixture is light and fluffy. Beat in the eggs one at a time, beating well after each addition. Reduce the speed to low and add the flour mixture alternately with the milk in 3 batches, beginning and ending with the flour mixture and beating just until blended. Beat in 2 teaspoons of the zest and the vanilla. Gently stir in the berries. Transfer the batter to the pan and smooth the top with a rubber spatula.

STEP 5: Bake for 1 hour and 30 to 40 minutes, or until the cake begins to pull away from the sides of the pan and a wooden pick inserted in the center comes out clean. Let the cake cool in the pan on a wire rack for 20 minutes, then turn it out onto the rack and set it right side up.

STEP 6: Meanwhile, bring the remaining ½ cup sugar, 2 teaspoons zest, and the lime juice to a boil in a small saucepan over medium heat. Remove from the heat and let stand for 5 minutes.

STEP 7: Brush the lime juice mixture over the warm cake and let cool completely. Serve, cut into wedges.

Rosemary, rose, and blackberry cake

Because of the whipped egg whites, this cake has a very delicate texture, which makes it a great tea cake. Or espresso cake. Because it's very tender, cut it carefully with a serrated knife. Rose water is available in specialty foods stores and many supermarkets.

SERVES 8

½ cup plus 2 tablespoons	**yellow or white cornmeal**
1 cup	**sifted cake flour (not self-rising)**
½ teaspoon	**cream of tartar**
¼ teaspoon	**baking soda**
¼ teaspoon	**salt**
1 cup (2 sticks)	**unsalted butter, at room temperature**
1 cup	**sugar**
1 tablespoon	**rose water**
1½ teaspoons	**finely chopped fresh rosemary**
½ teaspoon	**pure vanilla extract**
4	**large eggs, separated**
½ cup	**crème fraîche, homemade (page 153) or store-bought, or sour cream**
One ½-pint	**ripe blackberries**

STEP 1: Position a rack in the middle of the oven and preheat the oven to 325°F. Butter a 9-by-5-inch loaf pan, coat with 2 tablespoons of the cornmeal, and shake out the excess.

STEP 2: Whisk together the flour, the remaining ½ cup cornmeal, the cream of tartar, baking soda, and salt in a medium bowl.

STEP 3: Beat together the butter, sugar, rose water, rosemary, and vanilla with an electric mixer on medium-high speed in a large bowl until light and fluffy. Beat in the egg yolks one at a time, beating well after each addition. Beat in the crème fraîche just until blended. Whisk in the flour mixture just until blended.

STEP 4: Beat the egg whites with clean beaters on medium-high speed in a large clean bowl until they form stiff peaks when the beaters are lifted. With a rubber spatula, fold one-quarter of the egg whites into the batter to lighten it. Fold in the remaining whites just until blended. Then fold in the blackberries. Transfer the batter to the pan and smooth the top with a rubber spatula.

STEP 5: Bake for 60 to 65 minutes, or until a wooden pick inserted in the center comes out clean. Cool in the pan on a wire rack for 20 minutes, then gently turn out the cake and set it right side up. Let cool completely on the rack.

STEP 6: To serve, use a sharp serrated knife to cut the cake into slices.

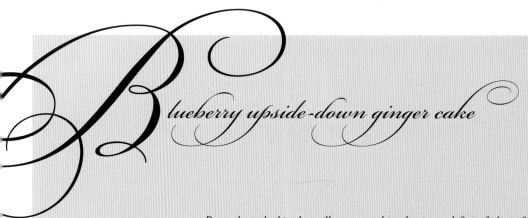

Blueberry upside-down ginger cake

*Down-home looking but still gorgeous, this cake gives a definite feeling of comfort.
You might want to serve this with crème fraîche instead of the optional ice cream,
but the ice cream does add a great temperature contrast.*

SERVES 8 TO 10

1½ cups	**all-purpose flour**
1½ teaspoons	**ground ginger**
1 teaspoon	**baking soda**
1 teaspoon	**ground cinnamon**
½ teaspoon	**ground cloves**
½ teaspoon	**salt**
¾ cup (1½ sticks)	**unsalted butter, at room temperature**
¾ cup	**packed dark brown sugar**
1 tablespoon	**fresh lemon juice**
1 pint	**ripe blueberries, picked over**
½ cup	**granulated sugar**
½ cup	**unsulphured molasses**
2	**large eggs, at room temperature**
¼ cup	**whole milk, at room temperature**
	Luscious Raspberry Ice Cream (page 126) or 1 quart vanilla ice cream (optional)

Continued

*Blueberry Upside-Down
Ginger Cake*

STEP 1: Position a rack in the middle of the oven and preheat the oven to 350°F.

STEP 2: Whisk together the flour, ginger, baking soda, cinnamon, cloves, and salt in a medium bowl.

STEP 3: Melt ¼ cup of the butter in a small saucepan. Pour into a 9-by-2-inch round cake pan. Stir in the brown sugar and lemon juice until blended; the sugar will not dissolve. Sprinkle the blueberries evenly over the bottom of the pan.

STEP 4: Beat the remaining ½ cup butter with an electric mixer on medium-high speed in a large bowl until light and fluffy. Add the granulated sugar and beat until light and fluffy. Beat in the molasses until blended. Add the eggs one at a time, beating well after each addition and scraping down the sides of the bowl with a rubber spatula as necessary. Whisk in half of the flour mixture. Whisk in the milk and then the remaining flour mixture. Transfer the batter to the pan and smooth the top with a rubber spatula.

STEP 5: Bake for 60 to 65 minutes, or until a wooden pick inserted in the center comes out clean. Cool the cake in the pan on a wire rack for 15 minutes. Run a table knife around the inside of the pan and invert the cake onto a serving plate. (Or if you want to serve the cake up to 1 hour later, leave the cake in the pan until ready to serve to keep it warm.)

STEP 6: Serve warm, cut into wedges, with the ice cream, if using.

Pies, tarts, and a cheesecake

I'm crazy about berry pies and tarts. For me, they are one of the very best ways to highlight berries in desserts. I love crust, I love berries, and I love the combination. I have always preferred crust to cake, but even more so when berries are involved. If you want an undemanding but dramatic spring or summertime dessert, make the Strawberry Sunburst Tart (page 40). It's a shortbread cookie crust topped with raspberry curd folded into whipped cream, topped with gorgeous strawberries, and finished with more of the luscious pink cream piped between the berries and around the edge. Strawberries are also showcased in the very French and totally elegant Square Strawberry Puff Pastry Tart (page 49)—you'll love it. Want a killer cheesecake? The Blueberry Cheesecake with Raspberry Curd (page 58) has a shortbread crumb crust, a lemony blueberry filling, and a topping of raspberry curd.

What's my favorite classic all-American pie? Keep the apple pie and give me a Double-Crust Blueberry Pie (page 52). It's a perfect contrast of textures—I love the pop and deep flavor of the blueberries against the crisp buttery crust, and

served with raspberry ice cream—it's my idea of heaven. One of my favorite people is Marie Simmons, and I'm offering you Marie's Blueberry Tart (page 43); you'll thank me for it. Make it with any berries you choose (except strawberries) and you will not be disappointed. Another great pal of mine, Carol Prager, baker extraordinaire, lent me her Strawberry-Rhubarb Lattice Pie (page 55) to share with you. It's exceptional and really shows off the classic combination of strawberry and rhubarb. I am a huge chocolate fan (as you may know) and one of my favorite things on earth is a chocolate tart. You'll find the Raspberry Truffle Tart (page 46) perfect in its simplicity, and it offers everything that's great about a chocolate tart—with the addition of fresh raspberries.

Strawberry sunburst tart

This tart is really spectacular. It looks stunning and I love its big flavors and contrasting textures. The crisp, sandy, sweet shortbread crust is filled with a blend of whipped cream and raspberry curd. Then the tart is topped with strawberries, and more of the curd mixture is piped between the berries and around the edge of the tart. This dough is very easy to work with, and the tart looks like a big round sun, with points radiating out like the sun's rays.

SERVES 8

	Pastry
2 cups	**all-purpose flour**
¾ cup (1½ sticks)	**cold unsalted butter, cut into small pieces**
½ cup	**confectioners' sugar**
¼ teaspoon	**salt**
¼ cup	**crème fraîche, homemade (page 153) or store-bought, or sour cream**
1	**large egg yolk**
½ teaspoon	**pure vanilla extract**
	Filling
1 cup	**heavy (whipping) cream**
	Luscious Raspberry Curd (page 147)
1½ pints	**small ripe strawberries, hulled**

Continued

Strawberry Sunburst Tart

STEP 1: *To make the crust:* Pulse the flour, butter, sugar, and salt in a food processor until the mixture resembles coarse crumbs. Whisk together the crème fraîche, egg yolk, and vanilla in a small bowl, add to the flour mixture, and pulse just until the dough comes together when a small bit is pressed between your fingers. Shape the dough into a disk and refrigerate, wrapped in wax paper, for at least 30 minutes, or up to 2 days.

STEP 2: Place the dough on a sheet of lightly floured wax paper and lightly flour the top. Top with another piece of wax paper and roll out to a 12-inch round. Remove the top piece of wax paper, transfer the dough (paper side up) to a large baking sheet, and remove the wax paper. To make the sunburst points, hold the thumb and forefinger of one hand against one edge of the dough, and push the dough between them into a point with your other forefinger. Then repeat, working your way all around the edge of the dough. Prick the dough all over with a fork. Refrigerate for at least 20 minutes, or up to 2 hours.

STEP 3: Preheat the oven to 375°F.

STEP 4: Bake the tart crust for 15 to 18 minutes, until light golden brown. Let cool completely on the baking sheet on a wire rack.

STEP 5: *To make the filling:* Beat the cream with an electric mixer on medium-high speed in a large bowl just until it forms stiff peaks when the beaters are lifted. Whisk in the raspberry curd. Spread about 1 cup of the mixture evenly over the tart shell, leaving a 1-inch border around the edge. Spoon the remaining cream mixture into a pastry bag fitted with a large star tip, put it on a plate, and refrigerate until ready to use.

STEP 6: Arrange the strawberries, with the points up, close together over the cream mixture. (The tart can be assembled to this point up to 3 hours in advance and kept loosely covered at cool room temperature.)

STEP 7: To serve, pipe rosettes of the cream mixture between the strawberries and around the edge. With 2 wide metal spatulas, carefully transfer the tart to a large platter, and serve, cut into wedges.

The lovely Marie Simmons gave me this recipe a long time ago when we were both working on a Peace Table project in Brooklyn. Marie is a wonder in the kitchen, and the minute I saw this tart, I wanted the recipe. After I tasted it, I was begging. It is perfect, and would also be perfect if you used raspberries instead of blueberries. Marie arranges the top layer of blueberries stem ends down for a very professional appearance.

SERVES 8

Pastry

1½ cups	**all-purpose flour**
2 tablespoons	**granulated sugar**
½ cup (1 stick)	**cold unsalted butter, cut into small pieces**
1	**large egg yolk**
1 teaspoon	**pure vanilla extract**
1 to 2 tablespoons	**ice water, if needed**

Filling

¼ cup	**granulated sugar**
2 tablespoons	**all-purpose flour**
5 cups	**ripe blueberries, picked over**

confectioners' sugar for dusting
Luscious Raspberry Ice Cream (page 126)
or Raspberry Whipped Cream (page 149)
(optional)

Continued

Marie's Blueberry Tart

STEP 1: Preheat the oven to 425°F. Lightly butter an 11-inch fluted tart pan with a removable bottom.

STEP 2: *To make the pastry:* Pulse the flour and granulated sugar in a food processor until well combined. With the motor running, add the butter through the feed tube. Stir together the egg yolk and vanilla in a small bowl. With the motor running, gradually add the egg mixture and pulse just until the dough comes together when a small bit is pressed between your fingers. If it seems too dry, add cold water a little at a time and pulse; the dough should be crumbly but not dry.

STEP 3: Transfer the dough to the tart pan. Press it evenly over the bottom and up the sides of the pan; the dough will look rough.

STEP 4: *To make the filling:* Stir together the granulated sugar and the flour in a large bowl. Add half of the blueberries and toss to coat with the sugar mixture. Transfer the berries to the tart shell and top with any sugar mixture left in the bottom of the bowl.

STEP 5: Bake for 15 minutes. Reduce the oven temperature to 350°F and bake for 35 to 40 minutes longer, until the berries are bubbling and the pastry is golden brown. Halfway through the baking time, stir the berries and turn over any that have flour on them.

STEP 6: Transfer the tart to a wire rack and top with the remaining berries, pressing them gently into the hot berries. Let cool to room temperature.

STEP 7: To serve, dust the tart with confectioners' sugar. Cut into wedges and serve with the ice cream or whipped cream, if using.

aspberry truffle tart

This dark and lovely tart is adapted from a recipe in Bake It to the Limit, by Dede Wilson. It's like a big truffle with a luscious raspberry ganache filling and whole ripe raspberries in and above the truffle mixture. Scatter just a few raspberries for an elegant garnish, or use a few more to make a pretty pattern.

SERVES 10 TO 12

9 ounces	**chocolate wafers, broken into large pieces**
½ cup (1 stick)	**unsalted butter, melted**
Four ½-pints	**ripe raspberries**
15 ounces	**bittersweet or semisweet chocolate, chopped**
1½ cups	**heavy (whipping) cream**
pinch of	**salt**

STEP 1: Preheat the oven to 350°F. Butter an 11-inch fluted tart pan with a removable bottom.

STEP 2: Pulse the wafers in a food processor until finely ground. Add the butter and pulse until well combined. Transfer the crumb mixture to the tart pan and press evenly into the bottom and up the sides.

STEP 3: Bake for 12 to 15 minutes, until the crust is dry and set. Let cool on a wire rack.

STEP 4: Pulse 1 half-pint of raspberries in a food processor just until broken up. Pour through a coarse strainer set over a bowl, pressing hard on the solids to extract as much liquid as possible.

Continued

Raspberry Truffle Tart

STEP 5: Melt the chocolate with the cream in a medium saucepan over low heat, whisking occasionally. Remove the pan from the heat and whisk in the raspberry puree and the salt.

STEP 6: Scatter the second half-pint of berries over the bottom of the cooled crust. Pour the chocolate mixture into the crust and smooth the top with a rubber spatula, covering the berries. Refrigerate, tightly wrapped, for at least 6 hours, or overnight. Refrigerate the reserved raspberries for the garnish.

STEP 7: To serve, remove the side of the pan, scatter the remaining half-pints of berries over the tart, and cut into thin wedges.

This has all the elegance of a Paris pastry shop. Try to find an all-butter puff pastry; the flavor will be much better. (Dufour makes an excellent one that is sold in many specialty foods stores.) The smaller the berries are, the more elegant the tart is, and it will also be easier to eat with smaller berries. You might add orange liqueur or light rum to the pastry cream instead of the vanilla—use about the same amount.

SERVES 6

Pastry

1 sheet (about 8 ounces)	**frozen puff pastry, thawed according to the package directions**
3 tablespoons	**water**
1	**large egg yolk**

Pastry Cream

2	**large egg yolks**
¼ cup	**sugar**
2 tablespoons	**all-purpose flour**
1 cup	**whole milk**
1½ teaspoons	**pure vanilla paste or vanilla extract**

Glaze

¼ cup	**strawberry jam**
1 tablespoon	**water**
2 pints	**small ripe strawberries, hulled**

Continued

Square Strawberry puff pastry tart

STEP 1: *Take the pastry:* Line a heavy baking sheet with parchment paper. On a lightly floured surface, roll out the puff pastry to 1/8 inch thick. Using a ruler and a sharp knife, trim the edges to make a 10-inch square. Transfer the pastry to the prepared baking sheet. Using a ruler and a sharp knife, cut a 1-inch border around the square, but leave about 1 inch each of two opposite corners uncut.

STEP 2: Whisk together the water and egg yolk in a small bowl. Lightly brush the egg wash on the border, avoiding the cut edges and being careful not to let any drip down the sides. Pick up one outside point of the cut border and fold it across the square, aligning it on the opposite corner of the base. Pick up the other outside point of the cut border and cross over to the opposite corner of the base, aligning the edges. Press lightly with your fingertips to seal, and crimp the edges with the tines of a fork. Prick the base of the tart shell all over with a fork. Brush the rim with the egg wash. Refrigerate for 30 minutes.

STEP 3: Preheat the oven to 400°F.

STEP 4: Bake the tart shell for about 25 minutes, until golden brown. Let cool to room temperature on a wire rack.

STEP 5: *To make the pastry cream:* Beat the egg yolks and sugar with an electric mixer on medium-high speed in a medium bowl until thick and pale, about 8 minutes. Reduce the speed to low and beat in the flour just until blended.

STEP 6: Bring the milk just to a boil in a medium saucepan over medium heat. Gradually add the hot milk to the egg yolk mixture, whisking constantly. Return to the saucepan and bring to a boil, whisking constantly; boil for 1 minute. Transfer to a shallow bowl and stir in the vanilla. Cover with plastic wrap placed directly on the surface of the cream and refrigerate for about 3 hours, until thoroughly chilled, or for up to 1 day.

STEP 7: *To make the glaze:* Heat the jam with the water in a small saucepan over low heat, stirring occasionally, until melted.

STEP 8: Brush the bottom of the pastry shell with some of the glaze. Spoon the chilled pastry cream into the center and spread it evenly. Arrange the strawberries on top of the cream, with the points up. Brush the strawberries with the remaining glaze. (The tart can be stored at cool room temperature for up to 3 hours.)

STEP 9: Cut the tart with a serrated knife to serve.

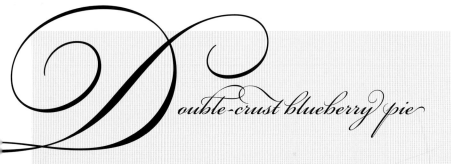

Double-crust blueberry pie

This was inspired by one of my favorite recipes published during the years I worked in the *Gourmet* magazine test kitchen. Originally developed by Amy Mastrangelo, it's a fabulous pie. I've changed it because I prefer cinnamon with blueberries. Don't use the very large blueberries here; wait until the height of the season and use tiny wild berries.

SERVES 8

Pastry

2 ½ cups	**all-purpose flour**
½ teaspoon	**salt**
¾ cup (1 ½ sticks)	**cold unsalted butter, cut into small pieces**
4 tablespoons	**cold vegetable shortening**
4 to 5 tablespoons	**ice water**

Filling

3 pints	**ripe tiny wild blueberries, picked over**
1 cup	**sugar, plus additional for sprinkling**
¼ cup	**cornstarch**
1 teaspoon	**finely grated lemon zest**
2 tablespoons	**fresh lemon juice**
½ teaspoon	**ground cinnamon**
½ teaspoon	**salt**
1 tablespoon	**cold unsalted butter, cut into small pieces**
2 tablespoons	**whole milk**

Continued

Double-Crust Blueberry Pie

STEP 1: *To make the pastry:* Whisk together the flour and salt in a large bowl. Cut in the butter and shortening with a pastry blender or 2 knives used scissors-fashion until the largest pieces of butter are the size of small peas. Stirring with a fork, add the water 1 tablespoon at a time, mixing lightly after each addition, until the dough comes together when a small bit is pressed between your fingers. Divide the dough into 2 pieces, one slightly larger than the other, and shape into disks. Refrigerate, wrapped in wax paper, for at least 30 minutes, or up to 2 days. (If the dough has been chilled overnight or longer, let stand at room temperature for 30 minutes before rolling out.)

STEP 2: Position a rack in the bottom third of the oven and preheat the oven to 425°F. Have ready a 9-inch pie plate.

STEP 3: Place the smaller disk of dough on a lightly floured sheet of wax paper, flour the top of the dough, and top with another piece of wax paper. Roll out the dough to about ⅛ inch thick. Remove the top sheet of paper, invert the dough into the pie plate, and remove the wax paper. Trim the edges, leaving a ½-inch overhang.

STEP 4: *To make the filling:* Toss together the blueberries, sugar, cornstarch, zest, lemon juice, cinnamon, and salt in a large bowl. Transfer the filling to the crust, mounding it in the center, and dot with the butter.

STEP 5: Place the remaining dough on a lightly floured sheet of wax paper, flour the top of the dough, and top with another piece of wax paper. Roll out the dough to a 13- to 14-inch round. Lay the dough over the filling and trim the edges to a 1-inch overhang. Fold the overhang under the bottom crust, press the edges to seal, and crimp the edge decoratively. Brush the crust with the milk. Cut 5 or 6 slits in the crust to let the steam escape, and sprinkle lightly with sugar.

STEP 6: Bake for 20 minutes. Reduce the oven temperature to 375°F and bake for 30 to 35 minutes longer, until the filling is bubbling and the crust is golden brown. Let cool completely on a wire rack.

STEP 7: Serve, cut into wedges.

Strawberry-rhubarb lattice pie

This recipe was given to me by Carol Prager—one of the best cooks I know. A classic, with perfectly balanced flavors and textures, this is really good, and it perfectly highlights the classic combination of strawberry and rhubarb.

SERVES 8

Pastry

2 cups	**all-purpose flour**
½ teaspoon	**salt**
¾ cup	**cold vegetable shortening**
5 to 6 tablespoons	**ice water**

Filling

1¼ cups	**sugar**
⅓ cup	**all-purpose flour**
¼ teaspoon	**ground cinnamon**
pinch of	**salt**
1 pound	**fresh rhubarb, trimmed and cut into ½-inch pieces (3 cups)**
1 pint	**small ripe strawberries, hulled and halved**
1 tablespoon	**fresh lemon juice**
2 tablespoons	**cold unsalted butter, cut into small pieces**
	Luscious Raspberry Ice Cream (page 126) (optional)

Continued

*Strawberry-Rhubarb
Lattice Pie*

STEP 1: *To make the pastry:* Pulse the flour and salt in a food processor until well blended. Add the shortening and pulse until the mixture resembles coarse crumbs. Sprinkle 1 tablespoon cold water over the mixture and pulse 2 or 3 times. Repeat the process with the remaining cold water as needed, 1 tablespoon at a time, following each addition of water by 2 quick pulses, just until the dough comes together when a small bit is pressed between your fingers. Divide the dough into 2 pieces, one slightly larger than the other, and shape into disks. Refrigerate for at least 1 hour, or overnight, wrapped in wax paper.

STEP 2: Preheat the oven to 425°F. Have ready a 9-inch pie plate.

STEP 3: *To make the filling:* Combine the sugar, flour, cinnamon, and salt in a large bowl. Stir in the rhubarb, strawberries, and lemon juice.

STEP 4: On a lightly floured surface, roll out the larger pastry disk to a 1/8-inch-thick round. Transfer the dough to the 9-inch pie pan. Trim the edges leaving a 1-inch overhang. Spoon the filling into the shell, top with any sugar mixture remaining in the bowl, and dot with the butter.

STEP 5: Roll out the remaining disk of dough to a 1/8-inch-thick round. Cut into 3/4-inch strips and arrange in a lattice pattern on top of the filling. Fold the edge of the bottom crust up over the ends of the strips, building a high rim. Seal and crimp decoratively. Place the pie on a baking sheet.

STEP 6: Bake for 15 minutes. Reduce the oven temperature to 350°F and bake for 45 to 50 minutes longer, until the berries are bubbling and the pastry is golden brown. Cool completely on a wire rack.

STEP 7: Serve, cut into wedges, with the ice cream, if using.

Blueberry cheesecake with raspberry curd

If you'd like, scatter a few ripe blueberries and raspberries over the cheesecake just before serving.

<table>
<tr><td></td><td></td><td>*Crust*</td></tr>
<tr><td>SERVES 10 TO 12</td><td>1¾ cups</td><td>**shortbread crumbs**</td></tr>
<tr><td></td><td>5 tablespoons</td><td>**unsalted butter, melted**</td></tr>
<tr><td></td><td></td><td>*Filling*</td></tr>
<tr><td></td><td>Three 8-ounce packages</td><td>**cream cheese, at room temperature**</td></tr>
<tr><td></td><td>¾ cup</td><td>**sugar**</td></tr>
<tr><td></td><td>3</td><td>**large eggs**</td></tr>
<tr><td></td><td>1</td><td>**large egg yolk**</td></tr>
<tr><td></td><td>½ cup</td><td>**heavy (whipping) cream**</td></tr>
<tr><td></td><td>1 tablespoon</td><td>**finely grated lemon zest**</td></tr>
<tr><td></td><td>¼ cup</td><td>**fresh lemon juice**</td></tr>
<tr><td></td><td>2 tablespoons</td><td>**all-purpose flour**</td></tr>
<tr><td></td><td>1 tablespoon</td><td>**pure vanilla extract**</td></tr>
<tr><td></td><td>¼ teaspoon</td><td>**salt**</td></tr>
<tr><td></td><td>1 pint</td><td>**ripe blueberries, preferably tiny wild blueberries, picked over**</td></tr>
<tr><td></td><td>1 cup</td><td>**Luscious Raspberry Curd (page 147)**</td></tr>
</table>

STEP 1: *To make the crust:* Butter a 9-inch springform pan. Stir together the crumbs and butter in a medium bowl. Press into the bottom and up the sides of the pan. Refrigerate until firm.

STEP 2: Preheat the oven to 450°F.

STEP 3: *To make the filling:* Beat together the cream cheese and sugar with an electric mixer on medium-high speed in a large deep bowl until light and fluffy. Beat in the eggs and yolk one at time, beating well after each addition. Beat in the cream, zest, lemon juice, flour, vanilla, and salt until blended. Gently fold in the blueberries. Transfer the filling to the crust and place the pan on a baking sheet.

STEP 4: Bake for 15 minutes. Reduce the oven temperature to 200°F and bake for 1 hour longer. Turn off the oven, open the door slightly, and let the cheesecake cool in the oven for 45 minutes.

STEP 5: Transfer the cheesecake to a wire rack and cool to room temperature. Wrap tightly and refrigerate until thoroughly chilled, at least 8 hours, or overnight.

STEP 6: Spread the raspberry curd over the top of the cheesecake. Refrigerate for about 30 minutes, until the curd is set.

STEP 7: To serve, run a table knife around the inside of the pan, remove the pan side, and cut into wedges.

Shortcakes

A whole chapter on shortcakes? You bet. Symbol of summer,
old-fashioned desserts, and maybe our very country.
There's more than one way to make a shortcake. First of all,
it doesn't have to be strawberry—any berry shortcake will be
a treat. Biscuits are my favorite type of shortcake base, and
maybe yours too, but I'd like you to taste the classic Piecrust
Shortcakes (page 68), made with crisp strips of pastry
and berries. I'm also very fond of the simple and homey
Boysenberry and Cardamom Toast Shortcakes (page 65).
A New England pleasure, Blueberry Gingerbread Shortcake
(page 78) takes you back to less complicated times and is truly
comforting. Chocolate Biscuit Shortcakes with Strawberries
Romanoff (page 73) offers chocolate lovers deep dark chocolate
biscuits and a refreshing mix of ripe strawberries and
orange flavors.

One Big Hazelnut Shortcake with Caramel Berries (page 70)
is a large and luscious hazelnut biscuit topped with berries
tossed with Berry Caramel Sauce (page 142). And shortcakes
don't have to be made with "plain" berries—try Strawberry and
Basil Shortcakes (page 75) or Roasted Strawberry Shortcakes
with Vanilla-Scented Biscuits (page 62). And the Easiest-
Ever Biscuits and Berries (page 80) is one of my favorite
combinations—very elegant as well as very easy.

Roasted strawberry shortcakes with vanilla-scented biscuits

This is my favorite strawberry shortcake. The delicate biscuits have a fabulous and unusual texture because they're made with whipped cream. They are topped with roasted strawberries and their syrup, and a garnish of heavy cream whipped with sour cream and sugar. It's a perfect celebration of summer and of life. Don't bake the shortcakes more than an hour ahead, though; they are really best made at the last minute.

Vanilla paste is a great thing. Rather than using just the seeds of a vanilla bean, you can buy a jar of the paste that's packed with the seeds and not have to waste anything. Nielsen–Massey makes a pure vanilla bean paste with beans from Madagascar, available at Williams–Sonoma and other specialty foods stores.

SERVES 6

1¾ cups	**all-purpose flour**
½ cup plus 3 tablespoons	**granulated sugar, plus additional for sprinkling**
1 tablespoon	**baking powder**
¼ teaspoon	**salt**
1½ cups	**heavy (whipping) cream, plus additional cream or milk for brushing**
2 teaspoons	**pure vanilla paste or vanilla extract**
2 pints	**small ripe strawberries, hulled**
½ cup	**sour cream**
2 tablespoons	**confectioners' sugar**

Continued

Roasted Strawberry
Shortcakes with
Vanilla-Scented Biscuits

STEP 1: Preheat the oven to 425°F. Butter a large baking sheet.

STEP 2: Whisk together the flour, the 3 tablespoons granulated sugar, the baking powder, and the salt in a medium bowl.

STEP 3: Beat 1 cup of the cream with an electric mixer on medium-high speed in a large deep bowl just until it holds soft peaks when the beaters are lifted. Beat in the vanilla. Make a well in the center of the flour mixture, add the whipped cream, and stir the mixture with a fork just until it begins to form a dough.

STEP 4: On a lightly floured surface, knead the dough several times, just until it is well combined. Pat it out to ½ inch thick. With a 3-inch cutter, crinkle-edged if you have one, cut out 6 rounds; gather the scraps together and pat them out again if necessary. Brush the biscuits with cream and sprinkle with granulated sugar. Place on the baking sheet.

STEP 5: Bake for 12 to 15 minutes, until golden brown. Let cool on the pan on a wire rack. Increase the oven temperature to 450°F.

STEP 6: Meanwhile, toss the strawberries with the remaining ½ cup granulated sugar in a medium bowl. Transfer to a baking sheet with sides. When the biscuits are out of the oven, roast the strawberries, stirring twice, for about 12 minutes, until soft and fragrant.

STEP 7: Just before serving, beat together the remaining ½ cup cream, the sour cream, and confectioners' sugar with an electric mixer on medium speed in a large bowl until the cream forms soft peaks when the beaters are lifted.

STEP 8: Split each biscuit with a fork and place the bottom halves on 6 serving plates. Spoon a generous portion of warm berries over each one, add a dollop of the cream, add the tops, and drizzle with the juices on the baking sheet. Serve immediately.

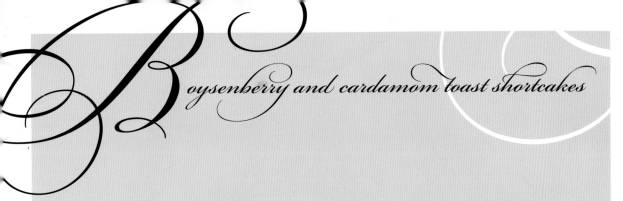

Boysenberry and cardamom toast shortcakes

The combination of cardamom and berries is one of my favorites. This dessert is very simple and homey, and I like the toast coated in butter and cardamom sugar much more than I do cinnamon toast. This is also very good with a mixture of berries, or with other blackberry relatives, blueberries, or raspberries. There's no need to thaw the frozen berries; just cook them a little longer.

SERVES 4

¼ cup plus 1 tablespoon	**sugar, or more to taste**
1 teaspoon	**ground cardamom, preferably freshly ground**
8 slices	**firm-textured homemade-style white bread**
6 tablespoons (¾ stick)	**unsalted butter, at room temperature**
Two ½-pints	**ripe boysenberries or 2 cups frozen boysenberries**
	Slightly Sweetened Whipped Cream (page 148; optional)

Continued

Boysenberry and Cardamom
Toast Shortcakes

STEP 1: Preheat the oven to 200°F.

STEP 2: Stir together ¼ cup of the sugar and the cardamom on a small plate, mashing any lumps of cardamom or sugar with a fork.

STEP 3: Toast the bread, in batches as necessary, until golden brown. Remove the crusts and generously butter both sides of each slice. Dip both sides in the sugar mixture to coat thickly and shake off the excess. Keep the toasted bread warm in the oven, right on an oven rack, while you prepare the remaining slices and cook the berries.

STEP 4: Heat the remaining butter in a medium nonstick skillet over medium heat. Add the berries and the remaining 1 tablespoon sugar and cook, stirring gently, for about 5 minutes, or until the berries are softened and heated through. Taste and add more sugar, if desired. Remove the pan from the heat.

STEP 5: To serve, cut each slice of toast diagonally in half. Arrange 4 triangles each on 4 serving plates, and spoon over the warm berries. Serve with the whipped cream, if using.

Piecrust shortcakes

I think this old-fashioned shortcake from colonial New England is a great idea. The strips of piecrust stay crispy and flaky, without getting soggy. As you can see from the ingredients list, the pastry is salty, and you can use less salt if you're skeptical, but I love the wonderfully salty crust in contrast with the sweet soft whipped cream and tangy berries. Serve this with warm pastry, if you can—just cut out the strips of pastry in advance and refrigerate them on the baking sheet until ready to bake. Roll the crust evenly so it bakes evenly. This is also terrific served with warm Blueberry Sauce (page 139).

SERVES 6

Pastry

2 cups	**all-purpose flour**
1 teaspoon	**salt**
½ cup (1 stick)	**cold unsalted butter, cut into small pieces**
5 to 7 tablespoons	**ice water**

Berries

2 pints	**small ripe strawberries, hulled and sliced**
	A double batch of Lemon Sugar (page 156)
	Slightly Sweetened Whipped Cream (page 148; optional)

STEP 1: *To make the pastry:* Whisk together the flour and salt in a medium bowl. Cut in the butter with a pastry blender or 2 knives used scissors-fashion until the largest pieces of butter are the size of small peas. Add the water 1 tablespoon at a time, stirring and mixing lightly with a fork after each addition, until the dough comes together when a small bit is pressed between your fingers. Divide the dough in half, shape into 2 disks, and wrap in wax paper. Refrigerate for at least 2 hours, or up to 2 days.

STEP 2: Preheat the oven to 425°F.

STEP 3: *To make the berries:* Stir together the berries and lemon sugar in a bowl. Let stand at room temperature until ready to serve.

STEP 4: Place 1 disk of dough on a lightly floured sheet of wax paper. Flour the top of the dough and top with another sheet of wax paper. Roll out to about ⅛ inch thick. Remove the top sheet of wax paper and, with a sharp knife, cut the dough into 1-by-4-inch strips. Transfer the strips to an ungreased baking sheet and prick each strip 3 times with a fork. Repeat with the remaining disk.

STEP 5: Bake for about 12 minutes, until lightly browned.

STEP 6: To serve, pile the pastry strips on 6 serving plates and top with the berries, and the whipped cream, if using. Serve immediately.

One big hazelnut shortcake with caramel berries

This dessert is dedicated the great state of Oregon, and all those growers of the best berries and fabulous hazelnuts, or filberts. You can use either room-temperature or warm (but not too hot) caramel sauce. If it's warm, be ready to serve the dessert immediately after stirring the berries and sauce together.

SERVES 6 TO 8

1¾ cups	**all-purpose flour**
½ cup	**ground toasted hazelnuts**
¼ cup plus 1 teaspoon	**packed light brown sugar**
1 tablespoon	**baking powder**
½ teaspoon	**salt**
1 cup	**heavy (whipping) cream**
3 cups	**mixed ripe berries**
½ cup	**Berry Caramel Sauce (page 142), at room temperature or warm**
	Slightly Sweetened Whipped Cream (page 148; optional)

Continued

One Big Hazelnut Shortcake
with Caramel Berries

STEP 1: Preheat the oven to 400°F. Generously butter a 9-by-2-inch round cake pan.

STEP 2: Whisk together the flour, hazelnuts, ¼ cup of the sugar, the baking powder, and salt in a medium bowl. Pour in the cream, stirring with a fork just until the dough comes together. (The dough will be very lumpy; do not overwork it, or the shortcake will be tough.) Transfer the dough to the pan and gently pat it out evenly with floured fingers (the top will be rough and lumpy). Sprinkle with the remaining 1 teaspoon sugar.

STEP 3: Bake for 30 to 35 minutes, until the top is golden brown and the edges are crisp. Cool slightly on a wire rack, then transfer to a serving plate.

STEP 4: Just before serving, gently stir together the berries and sauce in a medium bowl.

STEP 5: Top the shortcake with the berries and serve, cut into wedges, with the whipped cream, if using.

Chocolate biscuit shortcakes with strawberries romanoff

These shortcakes say CHOCOLATE! They have a rich, deep flavor and they're not too sweet. Because they are so dark, using a crinkle-edge cutter makes them look especially appealing. Sweeten the crème fraîche with a little sugar, if you'd like. Use the best cocoa powder available, and make sure it is Dutch-process.

SERVES 6

Berries

2 pints	small ripe strawberries, hulled and quartered
½ teaspoon	finely grated orange zest
¼ cup	fresh orange juice
¼ cup	confectioners' sugar
2 tablespoons	Grand Marnier or other orange liqueur
pinch of	salt

Biscuits

1 ½ cups	all-purpose flour
½ cup	granulated sugar
½ cup	Dutch-process cocoa powder
1 tablespoon	baking powder
¼ teaspoon	salt
¼ cup (½ stick)	cold unsalted butter, cut into small pieces
⅔ cup	half-and-half
½ teaspoon	pure vanilla extract
	Crème fraîche, homemade (page 153) or store-bought, or sour cream for serving

Continued

Chocolate Biscuit Shortcakes
with Strawberries Romanoff

STEP 1: Preheat the oven to 400°F. Line a large baking sheet with parchment paper.

STEP 2: *To make the berries:* Stir together the strawberries, orange zest, orange juice, confectioners' sugar, Grand Marnier, and salt in a bowl. Refrigerate, tightly covered, for 1 hour.

STEP 3: *To make the biscuits:* Pulse the flour, granulated sugar, cocoa, baking powder, and salt in a food processor until well combined. Add the butter and pulse just until the mixture resembles coarse crumbs. With the motor running, slowly pour the half-and-half and vanilla through the feed tube and process just until a dough begins to form; it will be very sticky.

STEP 4: On a lightly floured surface, knead the dough several times. Transfer to a lightly floured sheet of wax paper. Using a 3-inch cutter, crinkle-edged if you have one, cut out 6 rounds; gather the scraps together and pat out again if necessary. Transfer the biscuits to the baking sheet.

STEP 5: Bake for 12 to 15 minutes, until the biscuits are cracked and the tops feel dry. With a metal spatula, transfer to a wire rack to cool slightly.

STEP 6: To serve, arrange the warm shortcakes on 6 dessert plates. Add a spoonful of berries and a spoonful of crème fraîche to each, and pass the remaining berries at the table.

Strawberry and basil shortcakes

Even more than tomatoes and basil, strawberries and basil are my favorite summer flavor combination—and they make a great shortcake.

SERVES 8

Berries

2 pints	**small ripe strawberries, hulled and sliced**
3 tablespoons	**finely shredded fresh basil leaves**
3 tablespoons	**sugar, or more to taste**
1 tablespoon	**fresh lemon juice**

Biscuits

1 ¾ cups	**all-purpose flour**
1 tablespoon	**sugar**
4 teaspoons	**baking powder**
½ teaspoon	**baking soda**
½ teaspoon	**salt**
¼ cup (½ stick)	**cold unsalted butter, cut into small pieces**
¾ cup plus 2 tablespoons	**buttermilk**
1 to 2 pints	**vanilla ice cream**
1 to 2 pints	**strawberry sorbet**

Continued

Strawberry and
Basil Shortcakes

STEP 1: Preheat the oven to 450°F.

STEP 2: *To make the berries:* Stir together the strawberries, basil, sugar, and lemon juice in a medium bowl. Let stand at room temperature while you make the biscuits. Just before serving, taste and add more sugar, if desired.

STEP 3: *To make the biscuits:* Whisk together the flour, sugar, baking powder, baking soda, and salt in a large bowl. Cut in the butter using a pastry blender or 2 knives used scissors-fashion until the mixture resembles coarse crumbs. Make a well in the center of the flour mixture, pour in the buttermilk, and stir with a fork just until a dough begins to form; it will be very sticky.

STEP 4: On a well-floured surface, knead the dough very lightly once or twice with floured hands. Pat out the dough to ¾ inch thick. Dip a 2½-inch biscuit cutter into flour and cut out 8 rounds, reflouring the cutter as needed; gather the scraps together and pat them out again if necessary. Transfer the biscuits to an ungreased baking sheet.

STEP 5: Bake for 12 to 15 minutes, or until light golden brown. Cool slightly on the pan on a wire rack.

STEP 6: To serve, split each biscuit with a fork, and place the bottom halves on 8 serving plates. Spoon a generous portion of the berries over each one, place a scoop of the ice cream and sorbet on the side, and add the tops. Serve immediately.

Blueberry gingerbread shortcake

Not a typical shortcake, this is wedges of gingerbread topped with blueberries tossed together with a fennel–flavored sugar. The gingerbread is a cinch—just stir it together in the pan you bake it in. Serve this with raspberries or a combination of berries, or with another Fabulous Flavored Sugar (page 155), such as orange, coriander, or lemon. This is also good with sweetened crème fraîche or sour cream.

SERVES 8

2 pints	ripe blueberries, picked over
	A double batch of Fennel Seed Sugar (page 158)
1½ cups	all-purpose flour
¼ cup	packed dark brown sugar
1 teaspoon	ground ginger
1 teaspoon	baking soda
¼ teaspoon	salt
½ cup	apple or pear cider or juice
⅓ cup	unsalted butter, melted
¼ cup	unsulphured molasses
1 tablespoon	cider vinegar

STEP 1: Preheat the oven to 350°F.

STEP 2: Stir together the berries and fennel seed sugar in a bowl. Let stand at room temperature until ready to serve.

STEP 3: Sift together the flour, sugar, ginger, baking soda, and salt into an 8-by-2-inch round cake pan. Make a well in the center, pour in the cider, butter, molasses, and vinegar, and stir with a fork until smooth.

STEP 4: Bake for 30 minutes, or until a wooden pick inserted in the center comes out clean. Cool in the pan on a wire rack.

STEP 5: Serve the gingerbread, cut into wedges, with the blueberries on the side.

Easiest-ever biscuits and berries

These biscuits are great and they have only two ingredients! They can be made with sour cream, but I especially like them made with crème fraîche. They have an unusually light texture and a great tang that pairs well with berries. Because the biscuits look patched together if you gather the scraps together and reroll the dough, I just shape each biscuit by hand, so each one is perfect. There's no sugar in the biscuits, so you might want to go for the full two tablespoons of sugar in the berries, or as much as you think they need. Or use a Fabulous Flavored Sugar (page 155).

SERVES 4

Two ½-pints	**ripe raspberries**
1 to 2 tablespoons	**sugar, to taste**
1 cup	**self-rising flour (not cake flour)**
2 cups	**chilled crème fraîche, homemade (page 153) or store-bought, or sour cream**

STEP 1: Position a rack in the upper third of the oven and preheat the oven to 425°F. Butter a baking sheet.

STEP 2: Stir together the berries and sugar in a medium bowl. Let stand at room temperature while you make the biscuits.

STEP 3: Stir together the flour and 1 cup of the crème fraîche in a medium bowl with a fork just until a dough begins to form. On a well-floured surface, knead the dough several times with floured hands. Divide the dough into 4 pieces. Pat out each piece to about ¾ inch thick and, using a 3-inch cutter, crinkle-edged if you have one, cut out a round from each one. Transfer the biscuits to the baking sheet.

STEP 4: Bake for about 15 minutes, until lightly browned. Cool slightly on the pan on a wire rack.

STEP 5: To serve, split each biscuit with a fork and place the bottom halves on 4 serving plates. Spoon a portion of the berries over each, add a dollop of crème fraîche, and add the tops. Serve immediately.

A crisp, flummery, cobbler, grunt, buckle, and betty

These old-fashioned desserts are deeply satisfying in a basic, no-nonsense way. No, they don't have eight garnishes, as in posh restaurants, and they aren't fancy or impressive, but they are *good*. My Texas grandmother, Tressie, didn't make a special trip to the market every time she baked; she made do with fresh produce and the staples she always had on hand—flour, sugar, eggs, and butter. It's a style of baking that still makes sense today. These recipes are almost foolproof, but they do require juicy berries, bursting with flavor. Buy the best berries you can, and use them just as soon as you get them home. All of these are best served warm, and pouring or whipped cream or ice cream won't hurt either.

The Blueberry Cobbler (page 85) is a hearty, pleasing dessert that tastes as if your grandmother who loved you madly prepared it for you. The Strawberry-Hazelnut Crisp (page 87) is delightful and very comforting.

The Blueberry Molasses Grunt (page 90) is so wonderful
and old-fashioned you can imagine eating it while sitting
around a campfire. The Raspberry Buckle (page 92)
has a different kind of texture from the other desserts
here—it is a rich cake with a streusel topping, and lots of
ripe raspberries. Another simple pleasure, the Marionberry
Brown Betty (page 94), can end just about any dinner
with a cozy feeling. And you'll find the Blueberry
and Raspberry Bread and Butter Flummery (page 96)
irresistible—good buttered bread and berries baked
until they meld together in a delightful way.

Blueberry cobbler

Slumps and cobblers are both fruit desserts topped with biscuit dough and baked. The difference? A slump is topped with dropped biscuits, more like dumplings, and a cobbler uses cut-out biscuits. Both are traditionally served with heavy cream poured over the top. If you'd like to turn this into a nectarine and blueberry cobbler, pit and slice eight small ripe nectarines (you should have a generous 4 cups) and combine them with a pint of blueberries for the filling.

SERVES 6

Filling

3 pints	**ripe blueberries, picked over, or 6 cups frozen blueberries**
½ cup	**water**
½ cup	**sugar**
4 teaspoons	**cornstarch**
1 tablespoon	**fresh lemon juice**

Biscuits

1¾ cups	**all-purpose flour**
3 tablespoons	**sugar, plus additional for sprinkling**
1 tablespoon	**baking powder**
¼ teaspoon	**salt**
1 cup	**heavy (whipping) cream, plus additional cream or milk for brushing**

Continued

Blueberry Cobbler

STEP 1: Preheat the oven to 450°F. Have ready a 1½-quart shallow baking dish.

STEP 2: *To make the filling:* Combine the blueberries, water, sugar, cornstarch, and lemon juice in a large saucepan and bring to a boil, stirring constantly, over medium-high heat. Reduce the heat and simmer for 5 minutes, or until the berries are softened. Transfer the mixture to the baking dish.

STEP 3: *To make the biscuits:* Whisk together the flour, sugar, baking powder, and salt in a medium bowl. Beat the cream with an electric mixer on medium-high speed in a large deep bowl just until it holds soft peaks when the beaters are lifted. Make a well in the center of the dry ingredients, spoon in the cream, and stir with a fork just until a dough begins to form.

STEP 4: On a lightly floured surface, knead the dough several times. Pat the dough out to ¾ inch thick and, with a 2½-inch cutter, cut out 6 rounds. Gather the scraps together and pat out again if necessary. Arrange on top of the berries, brush with cream, and sprinkle with sugar.

STEP 5: Bake for 15 to 17 minutes, until the berries are bubbling and the biscuits are browned. Let the cobbler cool slightly, and serve warm.

Strawberry-hazelnut crisp

In the main, I don't care for cooked strawberries except in jam; I think they can lose their magic flavor, color, and texture—their soul. But that doesn't happen with this crisp. It's terrific, comforting, homey, and intensely strawberry, as well as buttery and rich, with lots of different textures. You might add minced crystallized ginger to the strawberries, and you might also make a double batch of Strawberry Whipped Cream *(page 149)* for a topping.

To make fresh bread crumbs, toss torn pieces of firm white bread or white sourdough into a food processor and pulse until you have coarse crumbs.

SERVES 8

3 pints	**small ripe strawberries, hulled and halved**
2½ cups	**coarse fresh bread crumbs**
½ cup plus 2 tablespoons	**confectioners' sugar**
½ teaspoon	**finely grated lemon zest**
¼ teaspoon	**salt**
½ cup	**chopped hazelnuts**
¼ cup (½ stick)	**unsalted butter, melted**
3 tablespoons	**granulated sugar**
1 cup	**heavy (whipping) cream**
½ teaspoon	**pure vanilla paste or vanilla extract**

Continued

Strawberry–Hazelnut Crisp

STEP 1: Preheat the oven to 375°F. Have ready an 8-inch square glass baking dish.

STEP 2: Toss together the strawberries, 1 cup of the bread crumbs, ½ cup of the confectioners' sugar, the zest, and salt in a large bowl. Transfer to the baking dish. Toss the remaining 1½ cups bread crumbs with the hazelnuts, butter, and granulated sugar in a medium bowl, and sprinkle evenly over the berries.

STEP 3: Bake for 40 minutes, until the berries are bubbling and the topping is browned. Let cool on a wire rack for about 10 minutes.

STEP 4: Just before serving, beat the cream with an electric mixer on medium-high speed in a large deep bowl just until it begins to thicken. Add the remaining 2 tablespoons confectioners' sugar and the vanilla and beat just until the cream forms soft peaks when the beaters are lifted.

STEP 5: Serve the crisp warm with the cream.

Blueberry molasses grunt

The story goes that when the berries bubble, their steam levitates the biscuit, and then
it falls with a sigh or a grunt. But it's just not an appetizing name, is it? I would have
chosen "sigh" for the name. The combination of molasses, blueberries, and brown spices
makes this a dish with the quintessential flavors of fall. This is also delightful prepared
with any variety of blackberry. (Raspberries are a little too delicate and strawberries
aren't good with the molasses.) Serve with heavy pouring cream or ice cream, if you'd like.

SERVES 6 TO 8

Filling

3 cups	ripe blueberries, picked over, or frozen blueberries, thawed
½ cup	sugar
¼ teaspoon	ground cinnamon
pinch of	freshly grated nutmeg
2 tablespoons	fresh lemon juice
2 teaspoons	unsulphured molasses

Topping

1¼ cups	all-purpose flour
1½ teaspoons	baking powder
¼ teaspoon	salt
5 tablespoons	cold unsalted butter, cut into small pieces
½ cup	whole milk
1	large egg, lightly beaten

STEP 1: Preheat the oven to 375°F. Butter a 9-inch deep-dish pie pan.

STEP 2: *To make the filling:* Place the berries in the pie pan. Whisk together the sugar, cinnamon, and nutmeg in a small bowl and sprinkle over the berries. Drizzle with the lemon juice and molasses.

STEP 3: Bake for about 7 minutes, or until the berries begin to release their juices. Remove the pan from the oven and increase the oven temperature to 425°F.

STEP 4: *To make the topping:* Whisk together the flour, baking powder, and salt in a medium bowl. Cut in the butter with a pastry blender or 2 knives used scissors-fashion until the butter resembles coarse crumbs. Stir in the milk and egg with a fork just until well combined. Drop the dough by the tablespoonful over the center of the berries; it won't cover them completely.

STEP 5: Bake for 20 minutes, or until the berries are bubbling and the topping is browned. Serve hot, warm, or cold.

Raspberry buckle

A buckle is a buttery one-layer cake made with fruit, often berries (especially blueberries), and sprinkled with a streusel topping. The cake rises and puffs up as it bakes, then it buckles. The result is a golden cake with berries peeking through the crispy topping. It's a celebration of textures, and I think it's especially luscious made with raspberries.

SERVES 9

Cake

2 cups	all-purpose flour
2 teaspoons	baking powder
¼ teaspoon	salt
6 tablespoons (¾ stick)	unsalted butter, at room temperature
½ cup	granulated sugar
1	large egg
1 teaspoon	finely grated lemon zest
1 teaspoon	pure vanilla extract
½ cup	whole milk
Two ½-pints	ripe raspberries
1 tablespoon	fresh lemon juice

Topping

⅓ cup	all-purpose flour
¼ cup	packed brown sugar
¼ teaspoon	ground cinnamon
¼ cup (½ stick)	cold unsalted butter, cut into small pieces

STEP 1: Preheat the oven to 375°F. Butter an 8-inch square baking pan.

STEP 2: *To make the cake:* Whisk together the flour, baking powder, and salt in a medium bowl.

STEP 3: Beat the butter with an electric mixer on medium-high speed in a large bowl until light and fluffy. Gradually add the granulated sugar and beat until light and fluffy. Add the egg, zest, and vanilla and beat until blended. Stir in the milk with a rubber spatula. Stir the flour mixture into the butter mixture with the rubber spatula; the batter will be very thick. Toss together the raspberries and lemon juice in a small bowl and gently stir into the batter. Transfer to the pan and smooth the top with the rubber spatula.

STEP 4: *To make the topping:* Whisk together the flour, brown sugar, and cinnamon in a small bowl. Cut in the butter with a pastry blender or 2 knives used scissors-fashion until the largest pieces of butter are the size of small peas. Sprinkle over the batter.

STEP 5: Bake for 30 to 35 minutes, until a wooden pick inserted into the center comes out clean. Cool in the pan on a wire rack for 15 minutes.

STEP 6: Cut the buckle into 9 squares and serve warm.

Marionberry brown betty

Some of the earliest Betties, in colonial times, were made in several layers with toasted bread crumbs, as opposed to just one of fruit with a topping. The lemon zest is also traditional (though I am crazy about lemons and berries). If you're using frozen berries in this recipe in particular, be sure to thaw them before mixing with the other ingredients; otherwise it's really difficult to blend them properly. I sometimes use mora, *a blackberry available frozen from Colombia, in this, but any blackberry cousin will be delicious.*

SERVES 6 TO 8

6 cups	**ripe marionberries or frozen marionberries, thawed**
½ cup	**packed light brown sugar**
1 teaspoon	**finely grated lemon zest**
2 tablespoons	**fresh lemon juice**
½ teaspoon	**ground cinnamon**
pinch of	**salt**
4 cups	**coarse fresh bread crumbs**
½ cup (1 stick)	**unsalted butter, melted**

STEP 1: Preheat the oven to 350°F. Have ready an 8-inch square glass baking dish.

STEP 2: Toss together the berries, sugar, zest, lemon juice, cinnamon, and salt in a large bowl. Transfer half of the berries to the baking dish.

STEP 3: Toss half of the bread crumbs with half of the butter and sprinkle over the berries. Top with the remaining berries. Toss the remaining bread crumbs with the remaining butter and sprinkle over the berries.

STEP 4: Bake for 45 minutes, or until the berries are bubbling and the topping is browned. Cool slightly, and serve warm.

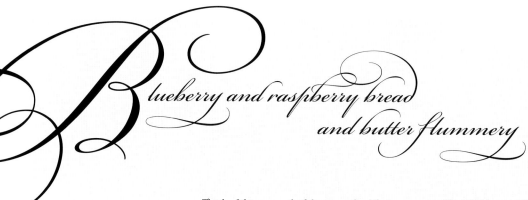

Blueberry and raspberry bread and butter flummery

Think of this as wonderful nursery food for grown-ups. If you'd like to make it even more adult, add a tablespoon or two of crème de cassis or other berry liqueur to the berries. It's very like an English summer pudding except that it's baked—a summer pudding needs to sit for many hours, and you can have this on your fork much sooner. It also makes a great breakfast.

SERVES 4 TO 6

2 pints	**ripe blueberries, picked over, or 4 cups frozen blueberries**
Two ½-pints	**ripe raspberries or one 12-ounce package frozen raspberries**
1 cup	**granulated sugar, or more to taste**
¼ teaspoon	**salt**
4 tablespoons (½ stick)	**unsalted butter, at room temperature**
8 slices	**firm-textured homemade-style white bread, crusts removed**
1 cup	**heavy (whipping) cream**
2 tablespoons	**confectioners' sugar**
pinch of	**freshly grated nutmeg (optional)**

STEP 1: Preheat the oven to 350°F. Butter an 8-inch square glass baking dish.

STEP 2: Combine the blueberries, raspberries, granulated sugar, and salt in a large saucepan and cook over medium heat, mashing the berries with a potato masher, for about 7 minutes, until the berries begin to soften and release their juice. Taste and add more sugar, if desired. Remove from the heat.

STEP 3: Generously butter each slice of bread. Line the baking dish with 4 slices of bread, buttered side up. Pour half of the berries over the bread and spread evenly with a rubber spatula. Add another layer of bread, buttered side down, and top with the remaining berries, spreading them evenly.

STEP 4: Bake for 20 minutes. Serve hot or warm, or cool to room temperature on a wire rack and refrigerate, covered, until thoroughly chilled.

STEP 5: Just before serving, beat the cream, confectioners' sugar, and nutmeg (if using) with an electric mixer on medium-high speed in a large deep bowl just until the cream forms soft peaks when the beaters are lifted. Serve the flummery with the whipped cream.

Puddings and a soufflé

There are times when there is no better dessert than a
soft, smooth pudding with berries. And here, for you,
is a lovely assortment. If you haven't ever had a classic English
Summer Pudding (page 101), you must—it is the very
essence of berries. Everyone loves custards and creams,
and sometimes it seems that the simpler they are the better,
such as the Vanilla Creams with Lime-Sugar Blackberries
(page 109). But then there are also recipes that are just
slightly more complex, like the Blueberry Marzipan
Custard (page 103), smooth and creamy and loaded with
blueberries. The Raspberry-Almond Clafouti (page 107)
is better even than the classic version made with cherries.
Who needs plain vanilla when there is Strawberry Crème
Fraîche Panna Cotta (page 104)? For your next dinner
party, make the Easiest Berry Terrine (page 115). It's
crammed with berries embedded in a berry gelatin, or
jelly, as they say in England, and it looks very dramatic,
and a lot more difficult than it really is, on a serving platter.
Blueberry Corn Custard (page 112) might sound a little

strange to you, but think about it—corn and blueberries
are at the height of their seasons at the same time and
both have a lovely sweetness. The Meringue Nests with
Raspberry Curd and Berries (page 117) are lush, crisp
brown sugar meringues topped with creamy raspberry
curd and fresh berries galore. And the Raspberry Curd
Soufflés (page 119) is the easiest soufflé recipe ever,
but very impressive, delicious, and fun.

English summer pudding

The English really know what to do with their berries, and this dessert is about as English as it gets. Feel free to change the proportions or types of berries, especially if you have a blackberry patch out back or some fresh currants on hand—just keep the total at about 3 pints. The juices from the succulently ripe strawberries and the sapphire luster of the blueberry juice soak through the bread and the result is a dessert that is the very essence of berry flavor.

SERVES 8		
	2 pints	**ripe blueberries, picked over**
	¼ cup plus 2 tablespoons	**sugar**
	½ teaspoon	**pure vanilla extract**
	One ½-pint	**ripe raspberries**
	1 cup	**sliced ripe strawberries**
	6 tablespoons	**unsalted butter, or as needed, at room temperature**
	10 to 12 slices	**firm-textured homemade-style white bread, crusts removed**
		Raspberry Whipped Cream (page 149) or Slightly Sweetened Whipped Cream (page 148; optional)
		Mixed ripe berries for serving (optional)

Continued

English Summer Pudding

STEP 1: Combine the blueberries with ¼ cup of the sugar in a large saucepan and cook, stirring, over medium heat until the berries begin to release their liquid. Increase the heat to medium-high, bring to a boil, and boil gently, stirring frequently, for 10 minutes, or until the mixture thickens slightly. Remove the pan from the heat and stir in the vanilla.

STEP 2: Stir together the raspberries, strawberries, and the remaining 2 tablespoons sugar in a bowl. Crush the berries a bit with a potato masher or the back of a spoon.

STEP 3: Line a 6-cup bowl with 3 sheets of plastic wrap, leaving a 6-inch overhang all around the edges. Generously butter the bread. Line the bottom and sides of the bowl with bread, buttered side up, cutting the slices of bread to fit.

Spoon the raspberry mixture into the bowl and smooth the top. Cover with a layer of bread, buttered side up, cutting the bread to fit. Add the blueberry mixture and cover with another layer of bread, buttered side down, cutting the bread to fit.

STEP 4: Fold the plastic wrap over the top of the pudding. Top with a plate slightly smaller than the bowl and weight it with about 3 pounds of cans or bags of food. Refrigerate for at least 10 hours, or up to 48 hours.

STEP 5: To serve, fold back the plastic wrap, invert the pudding onto a deep serving platter, and remove the bowl and plastic wrap. Serve with the whipped cream and garnished with the berries, if using.

Blueberry marzipan custard

Soufflé-like because it puffs, but not elegant and sophisticated like a soufflé—this is quite homey. Layered and intriguing, it is something like a clafouti made with marzipan and cream cheese. I love it with blueberries, but you can use whatever berries you'd like except strawberries.

SERVES 8

2 pints	**ripe blueberries, preferably tiny wild blueberries, picked over**
½ cup	**packed brown sugar**
One 8-ounce tube	**marzipan, cut into small pieces**
One 8-ounce package	**cream cheese, cut into small pieces**
4	**large eggs**
¼ teaspoon	**salt**
	Unsweetened whipped cream for serving (optional)

STEP 1: Preheat the oven to 375°F. Butter a 9-by-13-inch baking dish.

STEP 2: Place the berries in the baking dish and sprinkle with the sugar.

STEP 3: Combine the marzipan, cream cheese, eggs, and salt in a blender and process until smooth and creamy, scraping down the sides with a rubber spatula as necessary; it will take 1 to 2 minutes. Pour over the berries.

STEP 4: Bake for about 35 minutes, until golden brown. Cool slightly, and serve warm with the whipped cream, if using.

Strawberry crème fraîche panna cotta

You could puree a whole pint of strawberries and use ½ cup for the panna cotta, then sweeten the remaining puree and serve it as a sauce for the dessert. You do need a fine strainer to get the tiny strawberry seeds out, and make sure you use a large one, or the straining will take forever. With this and other berry desserts, the garnish of a different berry or berries from the type you've used in making the dessert is dramatic and gives a great feeling of abundance, as well as a fine and very fresh look.

SERVES 4

½ pint	ripe strawberries, hulled and halved
1 cup	heavy (whipping) cream
1½ teaspoons	plain gelatin
⅓ cup	sugar
pinch of	salt
½ cup	crème fraîche, homemade (page 153) or store-bought, or sour cream
1 tablespoon	orange flower or rose water, or more to taste (optional)
	Mixed ripe berries for serving (optional)

Continued

Strawberry Crème Fraîche
Panna Cotta

STEP 1: Puree the strawberries in a food processor (you will have about ½ cup).

STEP 2: Pour ¼ cup of the cream into a small heatproof bowl, sprinkle the gelatin over the cream, and let stand for about 5 minutes, until softened. Place the bowl in a larger bowl of hot water and stir until the gelatin has dissolved.

STEP 3: Meanwhile, bring the remaining ¾ cup cream, the berry puree, sugar, and salt just to a boil in a medium saucepan over medium heat. Remove the pan from the heat and whisk in the gelatin mixture, crème fraîche, and orange flower water, if using, until smooth. Taste and add more orange flower water, if desired. Pour through a large fine strainer set over a 4-cup glass measure, pressing hard on the solids to extract as much liquid as possible.

STEP 4: Oil four 6-ounce custard cups or 5-ounce ramekins. Divide the cream mixture evenly among the custard cups. Refrigerate, loosely covered, until set and thoroughly chilled, at least 3 hours, or for up to 1 day.

STEP 5: To serve, run a table knife around the inside of each custard cup, dip the bottom of the cup into hot water for about 10 seconds, and invert the panna cotta onto a serving plate. Serve immediately, with the berries, if using.

Raspberry-almond clafouti

A clafouti is not a cake, it's thicker than a custard, and it is most like a thick crêpe combined with a flan. A mix of berries is also nice here and you might like this even better with a light dusting of confectioners' sugar added just before serving. You'll get a smoother custard if you use a blender rather than a food processor.

SERVES 8

One ½-pint	**ripe raspberries**
⅔ cup	**crème fraîche, homemade (page 153) or store-bought, or sour cream**
⅓ cup	**whole milk**
½ cup (1 stick)	**unsalted butter, melted and cooled**
3	**large eggs**
½ teaspoon	**pure vanilla paste or vanilla extract**
¾ cup	**cake flour (not self-rising)**
½ cup	**sugar**
pinch of	**salt**
¼ cup	**sliced unblanched almonds**

Continued

Raspberry-Almond Clafouti

STEP 1: Preheat the oven to 400°F. Butter a 9-inch deep-dish glass pie plate. Place the raspberries in the pie plate, and set aside.

STEP 2: Combine the crème fraîche, milk, 6 tablespoons of the butter, the eggs, and vanilla in a blender or a food processor and process until smooth.

STEP 3: Whisk together the flour, ⅓ cup of the sugar, and the salt in a medium bowl. Whisk in the crème fraîche mixture just until blended. Pour the batter over the raspberries. Drizzle with the remaining 2 table-spoons butter, and sprinkle with the almonds and the remaining sugar.

STEP 4: Bake for 40 minutes, or until golden brown. Let cool on a wire rack for 10 to 15 minutes, and serve warm.

vanilla creams with lime-sugar blackberries

The lime sugar is great with the blackberries and the cool, smooth, sweet creams, but use any Fabulous Flavored Sugar (page 155) you'd like. I love using vanilla paste in these creams so they are flecked with the delicate vanilla bean seeds.

SERVES 8

2 pints	**half-and-half**
½ cup	**sugar**
pinch of	**salt**
3 envelopes	**plain gelatin**
1½ teaspoons	**pure vanilla paste or vanilla extract**
Four ½-pints	**ripe blackberries**
	A double batch of Lime Sugar (page 156)

Continued

Vanilla Creams with
Lime–Sugar Blackberries

STEP 1: Bring the half-and-half, sugar, and salt just to a boil in a large saucepan over medium-high heat; remove the pan from the heat. Sprinkle 1 envelope of gelatin over the mixture and whisk until the gelatin is dissolved. Repeat with the remaining 2 envelopes.

STEP 2: Pour the mixture through a fine strainer set over a large glass measure or a bowl. Whisk in the vanilla. Divide the mixture evenly among eight 6-ounce custard cups. Refrigerate, tightly covered, until set and thoroughly chilled, at least 2 hours, or for up to 2 days.

STEP 3: Toss together the blackberries and lime sugar in a medium bowl. Let stand for about 15 minutes, until the sugar is dissolved, or for up to 2 hours.

STEP 4: To serve, gently run a table knife around the inside of each custard cup, dip the bottom of the cup in hot water for about 5 seconds, and invert the cream onto a serving plate. Spoon the blackberries and their syrup around the creams and serve.

Blueberry corn custard

This luscious sweet corn pudding, although unusual, is a perfect dessert to serve when corn and blueberries are at their best. You might add a sprig of fresh basil or lemon verbena to the milk mixture while it's steeping for another layer of flavor.

SERVES 6 TO 8

1 ¾ cups	**whole milk**
1 tablespoon	**finely grated lemon zest**
¼ cup	**heavy (whipping) cream**
1 cup	**fresh corn kernels, preferably white corn**
2 tablespoons	**unsalted butter, at room temperature**
¼ cup	**sugar**
2 tablespoons	**all-purpose flour**
pinch of	**salt**
3	**large eggs**
1 cup	**ripe blueberries, preferably tiny wild blueberries, picked over**

STEP 1: Preheat the oven to 325°F. Butter an 8-inch square glass baking dish. Put on a kettle of water to boil for the water bath, and have ready a 9-by-12-inch baking pan.

STEP 2: Bring the milk and zest just to a boil in a medium saucepan over medium-high heat. Remove the saucepan from the heat, cover, and steep for 5 minutes. Pour the mixture through a fine strainer set over a large glass measure or a bowl, whisk in the cream, and let cool to room temperature.

STEP 3: Pulse the corn in a food processor just until coarsely chopped.

STEP 4: Beat the butter with an electric mixer on medium speed in a medium bowl until light and fluffy. Add the sugar, flour, and salt and beat, scraping down the sides of the bowl as necessary, until smooth. Add the eggs one at a time, beating well after each addition. Add the milk mixture and whisk until smooth. Gently stir in the corn and blueberries.

STEP 5: Transfer the mixture to the baking dish and place in the baking pan. Place the pan in the oven and pour enough boiling water into the baking pan to come halfway up the sides of the baking dish.

STEP 6: Bake for 55 to 60 minutes, or until the top is lightly browned and a knife inserted in the center comes out clean. Transfer the baking dish to a wire rack to cool slightly, and serve warm.

Easiest berry terrine

This simple but stunning terrine is delightful served with Strawberry or Raspberry Whipped Cream (page 149) or a dollop of crème fraîche, but it may possibly be even better with berry or other fruit sorbet. You could also use pomegranate juice (Pom Wonderful brand is excellent) or a favorite sweet wine instead of the cranberry juice cocktail. If you use strawberries, choose small ones and slice or quarter them. The terrine will slice better if you use smaller berries. My favorite berry mix here is a combination of tiny wild blueberries, raspberries, and blackberries.

SERVES 8 TO 10

2 cups	**cranberry-raspberry juice**
2 envelopes	**plain gelatin**
½ cup	**packed light brown sugar**
2 tablespoons	**fresh lemon juice**
5 cups	**mixed ripe berries**

Continued

Easiest Berry Terrine

STEP 1: Pour ½ cup of the cranberry-raspberry juice into a small bowl, sprinkle the gelatin over it, and let soften for 5 minutes.

STEP 2: Heat the sugar with ½ cup of the cranberry-raspberry juice in a medium saucepan over medium-high heat, stirring until the sugar is dissolved. Remove the pan from the heat and add the gelatin mixture and lemon juice, stirring until the gelatin is dissolved. Stir in the remaining 1 cup cranberry-raspberry juice.

STEP 3: Place the berries in an 8½-by-4-inch loaf pan. Pour the juice mixture over them and press the berries down so they are submerged. Refrigerate, covered, until set and thoroughly chilled, at least 3 hours, or for up to 2 days.

STEP 4: To serve, run a table knife around the inside of the pan and dip the pan in hot water for about 5 seconds, then invert onto a serving platter and shake to release the terrine. Serve cut into slices.

Meringue nests with raspberry curd and berries

Great textures here—the smooth and creamy raspberry curd, the juicy fresh berries, and the crisp meringues are terrific together. For a variation, fill the meringues with Luscious Raspberry Ice Cream (page 126) instead of the curd and top it with the berries. Fold chopped unsalted natural pistachios into the meringue for yet another texture.

SERVES 8	
3	large egg whites, at room temperature
¼ teaspoon	salt
⅛ teaspoon	cream of tartar
¼ cup	packed dark brown sugar
½ teaspoon	pure vanilla paste or vanilla extract
2 pints	small ripe strawberries, hulled and quartered
One ½-pint	ripe raspberries
3 tablespoons	granulated sugar
	Luscious Raspberry Curd (page 147)

Continued

Meringue Nests with
Raspberry Curd and Berries

STEP 1: Preheat the oven to 225°F. Trace four 3-inch circles each onto 2 sheets of parchment paper, leaving at least an inch between them. Place the parchment paper on 2 large baking sheets.

STEP 2: Beat the egg whites with an electric mixer on medium-high speed in a large bowl just until foamy. Add the salt and cream of tartar and beat just until the egg whites form soft peaks when the beaters are lifted. Push the brown sugar through a fine strainer into a bowl to remove any lumps. Gradually sprinkle the brown sugar into the egg whites, 1 tablespoon at a time, then continue beating just until the whites form stiff peaks when the beaters are lifted. Beat in the vanilla.

STEP 3: Spoon the meringue into the circles on the parchment paper, starting at the center and filling in the circles completely. With a tablespoon, shape each meringue into a nest.

STEP 4: Bake for 2 hours, or until the meringues are crisp but not brown.

STEP 5: Turn off the oven and let the meringues cool in the oven for 1 hour. Then cool completely on the baking sheets on wire racks. (The shells can be made ahead and stored in a tightly covered container for several weeks.)

STEP 6: To serve, stir together the strawberries, raspberries, and granulated sugar in a bowl. Place the meringues on 8 serving plates and top with the raspberry curd and then the berries.

Raspberry curd soufflés

The idea for this ingenious recipe comes from Sherry Yard, the pastry chef at Spago restaurant, where she makes her soufflés with lemon curd. Check out her book, The Secrets of Baking; it's brilliant. If you prefer more firmly set soufflés, cook these for the longer amount of time.

SERVES 6

¼ cup	sugar, plus additional for the ramekins
1 cup	Luscious Raspberry Curd (page 147)
2 tablespoons	fresh lemon juice
6	large egg whites
pinch of	cream of tartar

Continued

Raspberry Curd Soufflés

STEP 1: Position a rack in the lower third of the oven and move or remove the other rack(s) so there is at least 6 inches of space above it. Preheat the oven to 425°F. Generously butter six 4-ounce ramekins and coat them lightly but thoroughly with sugar.

STEP 2: Whisk together the raspberry curd and lemon juice in a large bowl.

STEP 3: Beat the egg whites with an electric mixer on medium speed in a large deep bowl until foamy. Add the cream of tartar, increase the speed to medium-high, and beat until the egg whites form soft peaks when the beaters are lifted. Gradually add the ¼ cup sugar, about 1 tablespoon at a time, and continue to beat just until the whites form stiff peaks when the beaters are lifted.

STEP 4: With a whisk or a rubber spatula, fold the egg whites, one-third at a time, into the raspberry curd. Spoon the mixture into the ramekins, piling it high in a dome shape. Transfer to a baking sheet.

STEP 5: Bake for 12 to 15 minutes, until puffed and golden brown on top. Serve immediately.

Frozen berry desserts

Berries make fantastic frozen desserts. Berry ice creams are terrific, and two of my favorites are Strawberry Crème Fraîche Ice Cream (page 124) and Luscious Raspberry Ice Cream (page 126). Neither are custard-based (they don't contain eggs), and I believe the berry flavors come through more clearly and they taste fresher and brighter. The Blackberry Frozen Yogurt (page 128) has a big berry flavor and another layer of zingy lemon, and the Blackberry and Raspberry Semifreddo (page 131) is elegant enough for the fanciest occasion. And I don't know a soul who would turn down Sundaes with Chocolate-Strawberry Sauce (page 130).

For an added treat, mix and match these frozen desserts with the sauces and toppings from the next chapter. The Berry Chocolate Sauce (page 144) or the Berry Caramel Sauce (page 142) are a good match for many of these confections.

Strawberry crème fraîche ice cream

I don't think there is a more classic combination than strawberries and crème fraîche, and together they make a remarkable ice cream. You'll love this with shortcakes or a baked berry crisp, or simply with ripe raspberries and blueberries tossed with a Fabulous Flavored Sugar (page 155).

MAKES ABOUT 1 QUART

1 pint	**ripe strawberries, hulled and sliced**
1 cup	**sugar**
1 cup	**heavy (whipping) cream**
1 cup	**crème fraîche, homemade (page 153) or store-bought**
2 to 3 tablespoons	**fresh lemon juice**
1 tablespoon	**pure vanilla extract**
pinch of	**salt**

STEP 1: Puree the strawberries with the sugar in a food processor. Transfer to a large glass measure or a bowl and whisk in the cream, crème fraîche, lemon juice to taste, vanilla, and salt. Refrigerate, covered, until thoroughly chilled.

STEP 2: Pour the mixture into an ice cream maker and freeze according to the manufacturer's instructions. After churning, the ice cream will be soft but ready to eat. For a firmer texture, transfer to a freezer container and freeze for at least 2 hours. This is best served on the day it's made.

Luscious raspberry ice cream

You'll find lots of uses for this. One idea—use the ice cream to fill the brown sugar meringues on page 117, and serve topped with Raspberry Sauce (page 138).

MAKES ABOUT 1 QUART

Four ½-pints	**ripe raspberries or two 12-ounce packages frozen raspberries, thawed**
1 cup	**sugar**
pinch of	**salt**
1 cup	**heavy (whipping) cream**
1 cup	**whole milk**

STEP 1: Pulse the raspberries in a food processor just until broken up. Pour through a coarse strainer set over a large bowl, pressing hard on the solids to extract as much liquid as possible. (You should have about 1½ cups puree.)

STEP 2: Add the sugar and salt, whisking until dissolved. Add the cream and milk and whisk until blended. Refrigerate, covered, until thoroughly chilled.

STEP 3: Pour the mixture into an ice cream maker and freeze according to the manufacturer's instructions. After churning, the ice cream will be soft but ready to eat. For a firmer texture, transfer to a freezer container and freeze for at least 2 hours. This is best served on the day it's made.

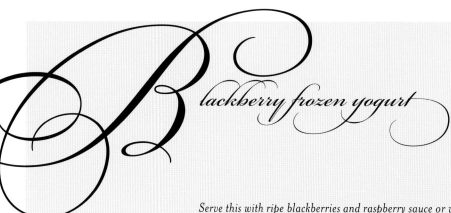

Blackberry frozen yogurt

Serve this with ripe blackberries and raspberry sauce or with blueberries and crème de cassis. For an elegant presentation, serve on very thin slices of cantaloupe and garnish with blackberries.

MAKES ABOUT 1½ QUARTS

2 cups	**plain whole-milk yogurt**
Two ½-pints	**ripe blackberries or one 12-ounce package frozen blackberries**
1 cup	**sugar**
1½ teaspoons	**finely grated lemon zest**
pinch of	**salt**
2 tablespoons	**fresh lemon juice**
1 cup	**half-and-half**
1 cup	**whole milk**
½ teaspoon	**pure vanilla extract**

STEP 1: Drain the yogurt in a fine strainer set over a bowl at room temperature for 40 minutes, or until you have about ½ cup of whey; discard the whey. Refrigerate the yogurt.

STEP 2: Cook the blackberries with the sugar, zest, and salt in a medium saucepan over medium-high heat, stirring frequently, for 15 minutes, or until the syrup is thick and the berries are very soft. Pour through a large fine strainer set over a bowl, pressing hard on the solids to extract as much liquid as possible. Refrigerate, covered, for about 1 hour, until thoroughly chilled.

STEP 3: Whisk together the blackberry puree and lemon juice in a bowl. Add the yogurt, half-and-half, milk, and vanilla and whisk until blended. Pour the mixture into an ice cream maker and freeze according to the manufacturer's instructions. After churning, the frozen yogurt will be soft but ready to eat. For a firmer texture, transfer to a freezer container and freeze for at least 2 hours. This is best served on the day it's made.

Sundaes with chocolate-strawberry sauce

Life would be better if we all ate more ice cream sundaes, especially ones loaded with chocolate and strawberry. This one includes alternating layers of a simple, very chocolatey sauce infused with strawberries and strawberry ice cream, and it's topped with toasted almonds, strawberry whipped cream, and a perfect strawberry on the stem.

SERVES 4

Berry Chocolate Sauce (page 144) made with strawberries

Strawberry Crème Fraîche Ice Cream (page 124) or store-bought strawberry ice cream

Strawberry Whipped Cream (page 149) or Slightly Sweetened Whipped Cream (page 148)

¼ *cup* **toasted sliced unblanched almonds**

4 **ripe strawberries on the stem**

STEP 1: Spoon about 1 tablespoon of the sauce into the bottom of each of 4 tall glasses. Add 1 scoop of the ice cream to each, then top with another tablespoon of sauce. Repeat with 2 more scoops of ice cream, alternating with 2 tablespoons of the sauce.

STEP 2: Add a dollop of the whipped cream to each sundae, garnish with the almonds and strawberries, and serve immediately.

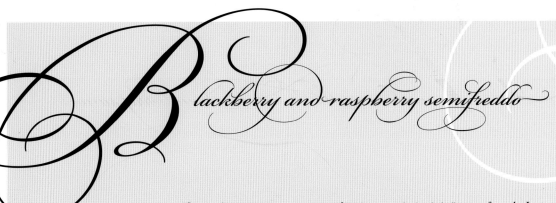

Blackberry and raspberry semifreddo

The word semifreddo, *pronounced "seh-mee-freh-doh," comes from the Latin,* semi *meaning half and* frigidus *meaning cold. This dessert is not semi-cold, though, it is semi-frozen. It doesn't freeze in the same texture as, say, ice cream or gelato, but in a softer, lovelier way—that just calls out for a spoon.*

SERVES 8

2½ cups	**ripe blackberries**
One ½-pint	**ripe raspberries**
1 cup	**sugar**
¼ cup	**water**
pinch of	**salt**
3	**large egg whites**
1 cup	**heavy (whipping) cream**
	Ripe berries for serving (optional)

Continued

Blackberry and
Raspberry Semifreddo

STEP 1: Line a 9-by-5-inch loaf pan with 2 sheets of plastic wrap, leaving an overhang on all sides to make unmolding easy.

STEP 2: Pulse the blackberries and raspberries in a food processor just until broken up. Pour the berries through a coarse strainer set over a bowl, pressing hard on the solids to extract as much liquid as possible.

STEP 3: Bring the sugar, water, and salt to a boil in a small saucepan over high heat, stirring until the sugar is dissolved. Boil for 2 minutes. Remove from the heat.

STEP 4: Beat the egg whites with an electric mixer on medium speed in a large bowl until foamy. Increase the speed to medium-high and, with the mixer running, slowly pour the hot sugar syrup into the egg whites, being careful to avoid the beaters. Continue beating for 8 to 10 minutes, until the egg whites are cooled to room temperature.

STEP 5: Beat the cream on medium-high speed in a large deep bowl until it forms stiff peaks when the beaters are lifted. With a whisk or a rubber spatula, fold the berry puree into the egg white mixture until almost blended, then fold in the whipped cream.

STEP 6: Spoon into the loaf pan and spread into the corners with a rubber spatula. Cover with the plastic wrap and freeze for at least 6 hours, or overnight.

STEP 7: About 15 minutes before serving, remove the semifreddo from the freezer. Fold back the plastic wrap, invert the semifreddo onto a serving platter, and peel off the plastic. Let stand for 10 minutes to soften slightly. Serve, cut into thick slices, with the berries, if using.

Sauces, toppings, creams, and a truffle

Sauces are a very important part of a berry dessert book, because often that's all you need to dress up any dessert. No other work necessary. A beautiful basket or two of berries and a drizzle of sauce are berries at their best. Most of the sauces and toppings here are made of berries, including Smooth Strawberry Sauce (page 136), Sliced Strawberry Topping (page 137), Strawberries with Balsamic Vinegar (page 137), Raspberry or Blackberry Sauce (page 138), Blueberry Sauce (page 139), and Sauce Cardinale (page 141), a thickened smooth strawberry and raspberry sauce. Then there are two slightly more complicated berry sauces: Berry Caramel Sauce (page 142) and Berry Chocolate Sauce (page 144). The Sauce Parisienne (page 140) is a berry sauce too, but it is prepared with strawberry puree, custard sauce, and whipped cream—an excellent combination. There are also the very flexible berry honeys and syrups—Any or All Berry Honey (page 146) and Any or All Berry Syrup (page 145). You'll find a luscious Custard Sauce (page 151) with lots of flavor variations

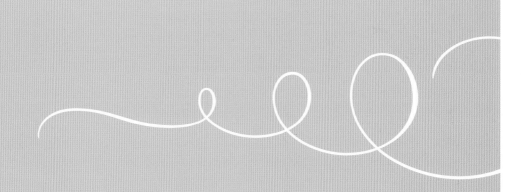

here too. Luscious Raspberry Curd (page 147) is an
ingredient in many other recipes, and it is great to have
on hand. There are also several whipped creams, a
Slightly Sweetened Whipped Cream (page 148), Strawberry
Whipped Cream (page 149) and Raspberry Whipped Cream
(page 149), and a Banana Whipped Cream (page 150) that
is fabulous and fun too. Follow the recipe to make your
own Crème Fraîche (page 153), and you'll find it comes in
very handy—it might be your favorite berry accompaniment.
You can make it all the way through berry season just
by using different Fabulous Flavored Sugars (page 155)
for your berry desserts—they're really indispensable.
If you make the Luscious Raspberry Truffles (page 160),
your life will be better, I'm sure.

Smooth strawberry sauce

Called a **coulis** by the French, this sauce is about as versatile as it gets.
Toss a spoonful or so of it with a bowl of mixed berries, top with a dollop
of crème fraîche, and Bob's your uncle.

MAKES ABOUT 2 CUPS

2 pints	**ripe strawberries, hulled and sliced**
4 to 6 tablespoons	**light corn syrup, depending on the sweetness of the berries**
¼ cup	**water**
2 to 3 teaspoons	**fresh lemon juice**
pinch of	**salt**

STEP 1: Cook the strawberries, corn syrup, and water in a large saucepan over medium heat, stirring occasionally, for 10 minutes, or until the berries are softened and have formed a sauce. Stir in lemon juice to taste and the salt.

STEP 2: Pour through a large fine strainer set over a bowl, pressing hard on the solids to extract as much liquid as possible. Serve warm, or cool to room temperature, transfer to a glass jar, refrigerate, and serve cold. The sauce can be refrigerated for up to 1 week. Serve chilled, or gently reheat before serving.

Sliced strawberry topping

This is the little black dress of the berry dessert world; you can use it over and over and over.

MAKES ABOUT 2 CUPS

2 pints	**small ripe strawberries, hulled and sliced**
¾ to 1 cup	**confectioners' sugar, depending on the sweetness of the berries**
2 to 3 teaspoons	**fresh lemon juice**

STEP 1: Stir together the strawberries, sugar, and lemon juice in a bowl. Let stand for at least 15 minutes to release the berry juices, or refrigerate for up to several hours.

STEP 2: Serve at room temperature.

Strawberries with balsamic vinegar

"As though they had been penetrated by the most ardent of summer suns," is how Marcella Hazen describes the taste of strawberries when you toss them with balsamic vinegar. Served at room temperature, this is lovely on its own, as part of a shortcake, or over gelato. Or try serving it on a bed of sweetened mascarpone, flavored with a little vanilla paste or extract, if you'd like.

MAKES ABOUT 2 CUPS

1 pint	**small ripe strawberries, hulled and quartered**
2 tablespoons	**packed light brown sugar**
2 teaspoons	**balsamic vinegar**
pinch of	**finely grated lemon zest (optional)**
pinch of	**freshly ground black pepper (optional)**

Stir together the strawberries, sugar, vinegar, and lemon zest and/or pepper, if using, in a bowl. Let sit for 15 minutes to release the berry juices.

Raspberry or blackberry sauce

Use any variety of raspberries or blackberries—including black raspberries, boysenberries, marionberries, or loganberries. You could also use mulberries, if you're lucky enough to have them. Delicious and versatile, this sauce is great to have on hand. Serve it with chocolate cake, brownies, or custard, or drizzle over ice cream, pound cake, or sliced mangoes, peaches, or pineapple. You'll think of plenty of other ideas.

MAKES ABOUT 2 CUPS

3 cups	**ripe or thawed frozen raspberries or blackberries**
½ to ¾ cup	**confectioners' sugar, depending on the sweetness of the berries**
2 tablespoons	**water**
pinch of	**salt**
1 to 2 teaspoons	**fresh lemon juice**

STEP 1: Pulse the berries in a food processor just until broken up. Sift the sugar over the berries, add the water and salt, and pulse once or twice. Add lemon juice to taste.

STEP 2: Pour the mixture through a coarse strainer set over a bowl, pressing hard on the solids to extract as much liquid as possible. Use immediately, or let cool to room temperature, transfer to a glass jar, and refrigerate, tightly covered, until ready to serve, or for up to 1 month. Shake well before serving chilled. The sauce will thicken a bit on standing; add water as needed to thin to the desired consistency before serving.

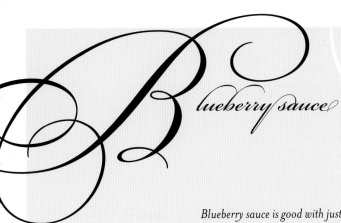

Blueberry sauce

Blueberry sauce is good with just about any fruit- or berry-flavored ice cream, gelato, frozen yogurt, or sorbet—and it's superb with vanilla and caramel ice creams.

MAKES ABOUT 1½ CUPS

1 pint	**ripe blueberries, picked over, or 2 cups frozen blueberries**
½ to ¾ cup	**confectioners' sugar, depending on the sweetness of the berries**
2 tablespoons	**water**
pinch of	**salt**
1 to 2 teaspoons	**fresh lemon juice**

STEP 1: Cook the blueberries, sugar, water, and salt in a large saucepan over medium heat, stirring occasionally, for 5 minutes, or until the berries are softened and have formed a sauce.

STEP 2: Stir in lemon juice to taste. Use immediately, or let cool to room temperature, transfer to a glass jar, and refrigerate, tightly covered, until ready to serve, or for up to 1 month. Shake well before serving chilled, or gently reheat before serving.

VARIATION: Add 2 tablespoons crème de cassis or other berry liqueur or berry *eau-de-vie* with the lemon juice.

Sauce parisienne

You'll love having this in your repertoire. It's very versatile and has only three ingredients—fresh ripe strawberries, whipped cream, and luscious custard sauce. Use it as a base for sliced strawberries or mixed berries. The recipe can easily be doubled.

MAKES ABOUT 1½ CUPS

½ pint	**small ripe strawberries, hulled and halved**
pinch of	**salt**
¼ cup	**heavy (whipping) cream**
6 tablespoons	**chilled Custard Sauce (page 151)**

STEP 1: Puree the strawberries with the salt in a food processor. (You should have about ½ cup.) Refrigerate, covered, until thoroughly chilled, at least 30 minutes, or up to 1 day.

STEP 2: Beat the cream with an electric mixer on medium-high speed in a medium deep bowl until it forms stiff peaks when the beaters are lifted. Whisk together the custard sauce and strawberry puree in a bowl; whisk into the cream. Serve immediately, or refrigerate, covered, for up to 2 hours before serving.

Sauce cardinale

Hull and slice a pint of small ripe strawberries, stir in about ½ cup of this sauce, and you've got dessert. (There's no need to add sugar.) The flavor is kind of a surprise—it looks like a strawberry sauce, but then you realize that it's also a raspberry sauce; it has endless uses. For a great whipped topping, whip a cup of heavy cream to stiff peaks, and beat in 6 tablespoons Sauce Cardinale, 1 tablespoon at a time. This recipe is an example of how well a potato masher, a very efficient tool, will serve you when making a berry sauce. Cardinale is the French term for food with a pinky-red tone, a color similar to the red robes worn by cardinals.

MAKES A SCANT 2 CUPS

1½ cups	**sliced ripe strawberries**
One ½-pint	**ripe raspberries or 1 cup frozen raspberries**
½ cup	**sugar**
1 teaspoon	**cornstarch**
pinch of	**salt**

STEP 1: Cook the strawberries, raspberries, and sugar in a medium saucepan over low heat, mashing the berries with a potato masher, until they begin to release their juices. Increase the heat to medium-high, add the cornstarch and salt, and bring the mixture to a boil, stirring. Boil, stirring, for about 1 minute, or until slightly thickened.

STEP 2: Pour the mixture through a large fine strainer set over a bowl, pressing hard on the solids to extract as much liquid as possible. Transfer to a glass jar and refrigerate until ready to serve, or for up to 3 days. Serve chilled.

Berry caramel sauce

Don't use a saucepan with a dark bottom, or it'll be too difficult to see the color of the caramel clearly. Hull and slice a pint of ripe strawberries, or use mixed berries, stir in one-quarter cup of the chilled sauce, and you've got an excellent dessert. You can use fresh or thawed frozen berries for the puree (you'll need about 2 ¼ cups berries for 1 cup seedless puree). The sauce may separate a bit in the refrigerator—just shake it up if you're serving it chilled.

MAKES A SCANT 3 CUPS

1 cup	**heavy (whipping) cream**
1 cup	**thick seedless berry puree (see page 22)**
2 cups	**sugar**
¾ cup	**water**
2 tablespoons	**light corn syrup**
pinch of	**salt**

STEP 1: Heat the cream and berry puree in a medium saucepan over medium heat just until hot. Set aside, partially covered to keep warm.

STEP 2: Heat the sugar, water, and corn syrup in a large heavy saucepan over medium heat, stirring until the sugar is dissolved. Increase the heat to high and bring the mixture to a boil, washing down the sides of the pan with a damp pastry brush if you see any sugar crystals. Boil, without stirring, until the caramel turns a dark golden brown, washing down the sides of the pan again with the damp pastry brush if necessary.

STEP 3: Immediately remove the saucepan from the heat and, being careful to avoid spatters, whisk in the cream mixture about 2 tablespoons at a time. Return the pan to low heat and cook, whisking, until the sauce is smooth. Remove the pan from the heat and stir in the salt.

STEP 4: Pour through a fine strainer set over a bowl, pressing hard on the solids to extract as much liquid as possible. Use immediately, or let cool to room temperature, transfer to a glass jar, and refrigerate, tightly covered, until ready to serve, or for up to 1 month. Shake well before serving chilled or gently reheat the sauce before serving.

Berry chocolate sauce

Use any berries you'd like here; raspberries are also particularly good. Drizzle this sauce over tarts, shortcakes, ice cream or sorbet, or baked berry crisps.

MAKES ABOUT 1¼ CUPS

¾ cup	**finely chopped ripe strawberries**
½ cup	**heavy (whipping) cream**
2 ounces	**bittersweet or semisweet chocolate, finely chopped**
1 tablespoon	**confectioners' sugar, or more to taste**
pinch of	**salt**

STEP 1: Heat the strawberries, cream, chocolate, sugar, and salt in a small heavy saucepan over medium-low heat, stirring and mashing the berries, until the chocolate is melted. Add more sugar to taste, if desired. Remove the pan from the heat and let stand for 10 minutes.

STEP 2: Pour the mixture through a fine strainer set over a bowl, pressing hard on the solids to extract as much liquid as possible. Let cool to room temperature, then transfer to a glass jar and refrigerate, tightly covered, until thoroughly chilled, or for up to 2 weeks. Shake well before serving chilled.

Any or all berry syrup

Add vanilla after cooking, if you'd like, or cook the berries with whole black peppercorns, coriander seeds, or a cinnamon stick. You'll find tons of uses for this syrup; I especially like it with a chewy meringue (see page 117) filled with strawberry sorbet. If you are using strawberries for the syrup, hull and slice them.

MAKES ABOUT 2½ CUPS

2 cups	**ripe or frozen berries**
1 cup	**water**
½ cup	**sugar**
½ cup	**light corn syrup**
1 to 2 tablespoons	**fresh lemon juice**
pinch of	**salt**

STEP 1: Bring the berries, water, sugar, and corn syrup to a boil in a large saucepan over medium-high heat, stirring until the sugar is dissolved. Continue to boil for 10 minutes. Remove the pan from the heat and stir in lemon juice to taste and the salt.

STEP 2: Pour the mixture through a large fine strainer set over a bowl, pressing hard on the solids to extract as much liquid as possible. Use immediately, or let cool to room temperature, transfer to a glass jar, and refrigerate, tightly covered, until ready to use, or for up to 2 months. Shake well before serving chilled or gently reheat before serving.

Any or all berry honey

I usually use a mix of berries here, but a single-berry honey is damn good too.
Toss the honey with fresh berries, or serve over ice cream, cake, or even waffles.
The honey makes a great gift, lasts a long time, and is delightful to have on hand.

Use a mild or a dark honey, whatever you like best. For a whipped cream with
a brilliant flavor and a lovely color, beat a cup of heavy cream to stiff peaks,
and beat in ¼ cup berry honey, 1 tablespoon at a time.

MAKES ABOUT 2 CUPS

1½ cups	**honey**
1½ cups	**ripe or frozen berries**
¼ cup	**cranberry-raspberry juice, white grape juice, or water**
Three 3-inch strips	**lemon zest removed with a vegetable peeler**
¼ teaspoon	**salt**

STEP 1: Bring the honey, berries, juice, zest, and salt to a simmer in a large saucepan over medium-low heat. Reduce the heat to low and simmer, mashing the berries and stirring occasionally, for 20 minutes.

STEP 2: Pour the mixture through a large coarse strainer (or a fine strainer if using strawberries) set over a bowl, pressing hard on the solids to extract as much liquid as possible. Let cool to room temperature, then transfer to a glass jar, and refrigerate. The honey can be refrigerated for up to 3 months.

Luscious raspberry curd

A curd is like a custard made with butter rather than milk, and this one is creamy, sweet, rich, and tangy from the berries and lemon juice. Use the berries of your choice here, depending on what you will be using it for. But for me, strawberries are too watery for good results and blueberries are too purple. I sometimes make a triple batch of this in a Dutch oven. Again, a potato masher makes quick work of mashing the berries.

MAKES ABOUT 1½ CUPS

½ cup (1 stick)	**unsalted butter**
Two ½-pints	**ripe raspberries or one 12-ounce package frozen raspberries, thawed**
5	**large egg yolks, lightly beaten**
¾ cup	**sugar**
pinch of	**salt**
2 to 3 teaspoons	**fresh lemon juice**

STEP 1: Melt the butter in a large saucepan over medium heat. Add the raspberries, egg yolks, sugar, and salt and cook, mashing the berries and stirring frequently at first and then constantly at the end, until thickened, about 10 minutes.

STEP 2: Pour the mixture through a coarse strainer set over a bowl, pressing hard on the solids to extract as much liquid as possible. Cool to room temperature; the curd will continue to thicken as it cools. Stir in lemon juice to taste. Refrigerate, covered, until ready to serve, or for up to 1 month.

Slightly sweetened whipped cream

Feel free to add 1 to 2 tablespoons crème de cassis, Chambord, or another berry liqueur, or an eau-de-vie. *Or try rose or orange flower water. You might even fold in very finely ground amaretti cookies. Or check out the Fabulous Flavored Sugars on page 155, and see what sounds good to you—lemon, lime, orange, cardamom, fennel, ginger, or coriander. I wouldn't use the mint or lemon verbena sugar—I don't want my cream to be green, not even on St. Patrick's Day.*

MAKES ABOUT 2 CUPS

1 cup	**heavy (whipping) cream**
1 to 2 tablespoons	**confectioners' sugar**
½ teaspoon	**pure vanilla paste or vanilla extract**

Beat the cream with an electric mixer on medium-high speed in a large deep bowl just until it begins to thicken. Add the sugar and vanilla and beat just until the cream forms soft peaks when the beaters are lifted. (The whipped cream can be made up to 4 hours ahead and refrigerated, tightly covered.)

Strawberry whipped cream

A great way to layer the berry flavor in a dessert is to use a berry-flavored whipped cream as a garnish; mix or match the berries.

MAKES ABOUT 1¾ CUPS

10	**small ripe strawberries, hulled and halved**
¾ cup	**heavy (whipping) cream**
1 to 2 tablespoons	**confectioners' sugar to taste**

STEP 1: Puree the strawberries in a food processor. Pour through a fine strainer set over a bowl, pressing hard on the solids to extract as much liquid as possible. (You should have about ¼ cup puree.) Refrigerate for 15 minutes, or until very cold.

STEP 2: Beat the cream with an electric mixer on medium-high speed in a large deep bowl just until it begins to thicken. Add the sugar and beat just until the cream forms soft peaks when the beaters are lifted. Slowly beat in half of the strawberry puree and beat just to stiff peaks. When serving, drizzle the cream with the remaining puree.

VARIATION

Raspberry Whipped Cream
Use ½ cup ripe raspberries instead of the strawberries.

Banana whipped cream

My great friend the late John Baran gave me this idea. It was from his childhood—first or second, I'm not sure. It's fantastic with strawberries.

MAKES ABOUT 1 CUP

1	**ripe (not overripe) banana**
3 tablespoons	**sugar, or more to taste**
1 teaspoon	**fresh lemon juice**
1 teaspoon	**pure vanilla extract**
½ cup	**heavy (whipping) cream**

STEP 1: Puree the banana with the sugar, lemon juice, and vanilla in a food processor, scraping down the sides of the bowl as needed. Taste and add more sugar, if desired.

STEP 2: Beat the cream in a medium deep bowl with an electric mixer on medium-high speed until it forms stiff peaks when the beaters are lifted. Gradually beat in the banana puree. Serve immediately, with fresh berries.

ustard sauce

There's nothing like berries and custard, whether you serve the sauce under, over, or around the berries. I prefer it under the berries or in a pitcher on the side; it pleases my eyes more. Feel free to vary the flavor by adding a liqueur—start with a tablespoon and add more to taste. Custard sauce is classically made with milk, but I find it better and more foolproof to use part cream and part milk. You can use all cream, all milk, or half-and-half, depending on your mood.

MAKES ABOUT 2 CUPS

¾ cup	**heavy (whipping) cream**
¾ cup	**whole milk**
4	**large egg yolks**
⅓ cup	**sugar**
pinch of	**salt**
½ teaspoon	**pure vanilla paste or vanilla extract**

STEP 1: Bring the cream and milk just to a boil in a medium saucepan over medium heat. Remove the pan from the heat.

STEP 2: Whisk together the egg yolks, sugar, and salt in a medium bowl. Slowly pour in the hot cream mixture, whisking constantly. Return to the saucepan and cook, whisking constantly, over medium-low heat for about 5 minutes, until the custard has thickened and coats the back of a spoon; if you draw your finger across it, it should leave a track. Do not let the sauce boil or scorch on the bottom; if tiny bubbles appear around the edges, remove the pan from the heat for a few minutes to cool the sauce and continue to whisk.

Continued

Custard Sauce

STEP 3: Immediately pour the custard through a fine strainer set over a bowl. Let cool to room temperature, whisking occasionally so it cools more quickly. Whisk in the vanilla. Serve immediately or refrigerate, covered, until very cold, about 1 hour, or for up to 4 days. (Reheat gently to serve warm, if desired.)

VARIATIONS

Raspberry Custard Sauce

Pulse a generous ½ cup ripe raspberries in a food processor just until broken up. After straining and cooling the custard, pour the berries through the strainer into the bowl, pressing hard on the solids to extract as much liquid as possible, and whisk together. Add the vanilla.

Fennel Custard Sauce

Bring the cream and milk to a boil, add 2 teaspoons fennel seeds, cover, remove from the heat, and steep for 5 minutes. Proceed with the recipe, omitting the vanilla.

Cardamom Custard Sauce

Bring the cream and milk to a boil, add 3 crushed cardamom pods, cover, remove from the heat, and steep for 5 minutes. Proceed with the recipe, omitting the vanilla.

Ginger Custard Sauce

Bring the cream and milk to a boil, add 3 to 4 tablespoons finely chopped crystallized ginger, cover, remove from the heat, and steep for 5 minutes. Proceed with the recipe, omitting the vanilla.

Bay Leaf Custard Sauce

Bring the cream and milk to a boil, add 2 imported bay leaves or 1 California bay leaf, cover, remove from the heat, and steep for 5 minutes. Proceed with the recipe as directed.

Saffron Custard Sauce

Crumble a large pinch of saffron threads with your fingers. Bring the cream and milk to boil, add the saffron, cover, remove from the heat, and steep for 5 minutes. Proceed with the recipe as directed.

Lime Custard Sauce

Bring the cream and milk to a boil, add 3 strips lime zest (removed with a vegetable peeler), cover, remove from the heat, and steep for 5 minutes. Proceed with the recipe, adding 2 to 3 teaspoons fresh lime juice instead of the vanilla.

Crème fraîche

Pronounced "krehm fraish," it is perfect with berries. Originally from France, crème fraîche is like a very refined sour cream—not quite as sharp and with a lighter, almost whipped texture. You can buy it, but I find it expensive, and since it's not available in my neighborhood, I prefer to make it. My favorite way is to culture heavy cream with store-bought crème fraîche and keep it in my refrigerator ad infinitum, like a sourdough starter. If made with ultra-pasteurized cream, it lasts forever, and when you get low, you just use it as the starter to make more. I do like to have it in the refrigerator waiting for me and my berries. Sweeten it with a bit of confectioners' sugar if you'd like, gauging it against the sweetness of the berries.

My second choice for making crème fraîche is a very thick, very rich Greek yogurt. A lowfat or no-fat yogurt just doesn't do it; neither does the commonly used buttermilk—it just doesn't get thick enough. Another great choice is sour cream with live cultures (and no bovine growth hormones), available in specialty and natural foods stores.

You can steep herbs in the cream while it's thickening if you'd like—whole bay leaves are perfect. Add two California bay leaves for this size batch, and serve it with ripe blackberries. Sweeten it with one of the Fabulous Flavored Sugars (page 155), if you'd like, or with granulated or confectioners' sugar.

Continued

Crème fraîche

Raspberry
crème fraîche

You'll need a generous quarter cup of ripe raspberries for the puree.

MAKES ABOUT 1 CUP

½ cup — **heavy (whipping) cream**

½ cup — **crème fraîche, Greek or regular whole-milk yogurt, or sour cream with live cultures**

Pour the cream into a glass jar with a tight-fitting lid and spoon in the crème fraîche. Let sit on the counter, with the lid slightly ajar, until the mixture thickens, from 4 to 24 hours, depending on the weather. Refrigerate, tightly covered, until ready to use.

MAKES ABOUT 1¼ CUPS

1 cup — **crème fraîche (left)**

2 tablespoons — **confectioners' sugar**

2 tablespoons — **seedless raspberry puree**

If the crème fraîche is not already thick, whip it with an electric mixer on medium speed in a large deep bowl just until it forms soft peaks when the beaters are lifted. Beat in the sugar and the raspberry puree. If the crème fraîche is quite thick, just whisk the ingredients together until combined.

Fabulous flavored sugars for berries

Older cookbooks often instructed readers to "put a vanilla bean in a jar of sugar and wait a month for it to flavor the sugar." Who has that time now? These "almost-instant" flavored sugars are a boon to busy cooks and berry lovers. Just hull and slice a pint of strawberries, or use a pint of your favorite berries, or an assortment, and stir in one of these flavored sugars. Let the berries sit for 10 to 15 minutes for the sugar to dissolve and the flavors to blend, and you've got dessert. Mash some of the berries, if that's your thing—some of us believe it makes berries taste better.

There are many ways to make these sugars, depending on the equipment you have. If you have a coffee or spice grinder, use it. It's the best method, because you get the finest result—it grinds the spices most evenly and finely—and you're making superfine sugar (which will dissolve most quickly on the berries) while you're at it. Or put the flavoring ingredients in a mortar and pestle (I use a large one from Southeast Asia) and add half of the sugar for the pounding, then stir in the remaining sugar. Or, you can simply stir the ground spices into the sugar in a bowl.

If you'd like, use confectioners' or brown sugar; confectioners' sugar will make a slightly thicker syrup with the juices of the berries (because it contains cornstarch), and brown sugar adds a caramelish flavor. Consider a combination of flavors—like mint and lime, ginger and orange, or vanilla and lemon. I'm including serving ideas here using strawberries, but you could substitute a pint of any berry you choose. You can also use these sugars to flavor whipped cream or a mixture of heavy cream and crème fraîche.

Continued

Lemon sugar

2 tablespoons	**sugar**
½ teaspoon	**finely grated lemon zest**

Process the sugar and zest in a coffee grinder until finely ground. Or pound half the sugar and the zest in a mortar and pestle until finely ground, and stir in the remaining sugar. Or stir together the sugar and zest in a small bowl until well combined.

SERVING SUGGESTION
Hull and slice a pint of strawberries, stir in the lemon sugar, and let stand until the sugar is dissolved and the berries release their juices. Serve layered with strawberry and mango sorbets in tall glasses.

VARIATIONS: For Lime Sugar, use a scant ½ teaspoon finely grated lime zest. For Orange Sugar, use ¼ teaspoon finely grated orange zest.

Mint sugar

2 tablespoons	**sugar**
4 to 6	**fresh mint leaves**

Process the sugar and mint leaves in a coffee grinder until finely ground.

SERVING SUGGESTION
Hull and slice a pint of strawberries, toss with cubes of fresh ripe pineapple and mango, stir in the mint sugar, and let stand until the sugar is dissolved and the berries release their juices.

Vanilla sugar

2 tablespoons	**sugar**
¼ teaspoon	**vanilla paste or a 1-inch piece vanilla bean, finely chopped**

Stir together the sugar and vanilla paste in a bowl until well combined, breaking up any lumps with a fork. Or process the sugar and vanilla bean in a coffee grinder until finely ground. Or pound half the sugar and the vanilla bean in a mortar and pestle until finely ground, and stir in the remaining sugar.

SERVING SUGGESTION
Hull and slice a pint of strawberries, stir in the vanilla sugar, and let stand until the sugar is dissolved and the berries release their juices. Serve spooned over toasted pound cake, angel food cake, or brioche—you could add strawberry or vanilla ice cream.

Cardamom sugar

2 tablespoons	**sugar**
	Seeds from 1 cardamom pod or a generous ⅛ teaspoon ground cardamom

Process the sugar and cardamom seeds in a coffee grinder until finely ground. Or pound half the sugar and the cardamom seeds in a mortar and pestle until finely ground, and stir in the remaining sugar. Or stir together the sugar and ground cardamom in a small bowl until well combined.

SERVING SUGGESTION
Hull and slice a pint of strawberries, stir in the cardamom sugar, and let stand until the sugar is dissolved and the berries release their juices. Serve over a custard sauce or lemon, chocolate, vanilla, or rice pudding.

Fennel seed (or aniseed) sugar

2 tablespoons	**sugar**
scant ¼ teaspoon	**fennel seeds or aniseed**

Process the sugar and fennel seeds in a coffee grinder until finely ground. Or pound half the sugar and the fennel seeds in a mortar and pestle until finely ground, and stir in the remaining sugar.

SERVING SUGGESTION
Hull and slice a pint of strawberries, stir in the fennel sugar, and let stand until the sugar is dissolved and the berries release their juices. Serve with dollops of sweetened Greek yogurt or fresh ricotta cheese.

Ginger sugar

2 tablespoons	**sugar**
	A quarter-size piece of crystallized ginger

Process the sugar and ginger in a coffee grinder until finely ground. Or pound half the sugar and the ginger in a mortar and pestle until finely ground, and stir in the remaining sugar.

SERVING SUGGESTION
Hull and slice a pint of strawberries, stir in the ginger sugar, and let stand until the sugar is dissolved and the berries release their juices. Serve spooned over brownies or meringues, with whipped cream, if you'd like.

Coriander sugar

| 2 tablespoons | sugar |
| ¼ teaspoon | coriander seeds or ground coriander |

Process the sugar and coriander seeds in a coffee grinder until finely ground. Or pound half the sugar and the coriander seeds in a mortar and pestle until finely ground, and stir in the remaining sugar. Or stir together the sugar and ground coriander in a small bowl until well combined.

SERVING SUGGESTION

Hull and slice a pint of strawberries, stir in the coriander sugar, and let stand until the sugar is dissolved and the berries release their juices. Serve with slices of warm gingerbread.

Lemon verbena sugar

| 2 tablespoons | sugar |
| 4 to 6 | fresh lemon verbena leaves |

Process the sugar and lemon verbena together in a coffee grinder until finely ground.

SERVING SUGGESTION

Hull and slice a pint of strawberries, stir in the lemon verbena sugar, and let stand until the sugar is dissolved and the berries release their juices. Toss with a handful of raspberries and blueberries and serve topped with Strawberry Whipped Cream (page 149).

Luscious raspberry truffles

A rich chocolate ganache combined with a puree of ripe fresh raspberries makes a lovely truffle—so nice to have around the house. These freeze beautifully—just roll, place them on a baking sheet, and freeze, then toss into a self-sealing bag or pack in a tin. When you want to serve them, defrost, roll in the cocoa, and let come to room temperature.

MAKES ABOUT
4 DOZEN TRUFFLES

One ½-pint	**ripe raspberries or 1 cup frozen raspberries, thawed**
2 tablespoons	**crème de cassis or other berry liqueur (optional)**
pinch of	**salt**
1¼ cups	**heavy (whipping) cream**
1 pound	**bittersweet or semisweet chocolate, finely chopped**
½ cup	**unsweetened cocoa powder**

STEP 1: Pulse the raspberries, crème de cassis, if using, and salt in a food processor just until the berries are broken up. Pour through a coarse strainer set over a bowl, pressing hard on the solids to extract as much liquid as possible.

STEP 2: Bring the cream just to a boil in a medium saucepan over medium heat. Remove the pan from the heat, add the chocolate, and whisk until smooth. Pour the mixture into a bowl and let cool to room temperature.

STEP 3: Whisk the raspberry mixture into the chocolate mixture. Refrigerate, covered, for 2 to 3 hours, until firm and thoroughly chilled.

STEP 4: Place the cocoa in a shallow bowl. Working quickly, roll a rounded measuring teaspoon of the chocolate mixture to a 1-inch ball in your hands, lightly coat with the cocoa, and set on a plate. Repeat with the remaining truffle mixture and cocoa. Store in an airtight container in the refrigerator between layers of wax paper for up to 1 week. Serve at room temperature.

Table of equivalents

The exact equivalents in the following tables have been rounded for convenience.

LIQUID / DRY MEASURES

U.S.	Metric
¼ teaspoon	1.25 milliliters
½ teaspoon	2.5 milliliters
1 teaspoon	5 milliliters
1 tablespoon (3 teaspoons)	15 milliliters
1 fluid ounce (2 tablespoons)	30 milliliters
¼ cup	60 milliliters
⅓ cup	80 milliliters
½ cup	120 milliliters
1 cup	240 milliliters
1 pint (2 cups)	480 milliliters
1 quart (4 cups, 32 ounces)	960 milliliters
1 gallon (4 quarts)	3.84 liters
1 ounce (by weight)	28 grams
1 pound	454 grams
2.2 pounds	1 kilogram

LENGTH

U.S.	Metric
⅛ inch	3 millimeters
¼ inch	6 millimeters
½ inch	12 millimeters
1 inch	2.5 centimeters

OVEN TEMPERATURE

Fahrenheit	Celsius	Gas
250	120	½
275	140	1
300	150	2
325	160	3
350	180	4
375	190	5
400	200	6
425	220	7
450	230	8
475	240	9
500	260	10